MW00667895

"Courageous Woman, Live Your Inner Power will help women to look inward and find peace in a world that bombards them with messages to put others first. This is for any woman who is tired of settling."

> ~ **Rachael Jayne Groover,** Best-selling author of *Powerful and Feminine.* Creator of *Art of Feminine Presence trainings.*

"After more than 30 years of personal and spiritual development, it's clear to me that Laurel's Inner Power Wheel represents a natural, divine process within each human for accessing and engaging our greatest power. Bring the wheel into focus, activate it and watch the magic unfold. I am excited to put the wheel into conscious practice and experience my next level of transformation!"

> ~ **Pixie Hamilton,** Civil Engineer for the U.S. Geological Survey, Department of Interior

"Indeed a book about Courage and true Power! Laurel Holland has brought a clear pathway for spiritual growth, self understanding, and deep inner joy. I recommend this book for those who know there is more to life, and are ready to find it."

> ~ **Kinlen Wheeler,** Co-Creator of Sacred Pathways

"For anyone who longs to find, touch, or explore the unending ribbon of answers waiting for you within your being... This book is a treasure; it's like an intimate conversation with a good friend. Laurel's words are a gentle invitation to the unfolding of your healing and a gift to read on every page."

> ~ **Rachel Camfield,** Southeast Sales + Media Ambassador at catstudio

"Courageous Woman, Live Your Inner Power takes a profound process and delivers it in a practical and simple way. This book is a must for any woman who wants to address her fears and insecurities."

> ~ **Coco Crissey,** Business Coach and Creator of Heartfelt Wealth

Courageous Woman

LIVE YOUR INNER POWER

LAUREL HOLLAND

To Jean -
I'm so glad we
reconnected! You are a
light - Keep shining that
beauty - Much love,
Laurel

COURAGEOUS WOMAN

LIVE

YOUR

INNER

POWER

LAUREL HOLLAND

Wild
ginger
Press

ISBN: 978-0-9960785-7-3

Cover image: Dustin Neece © 2014, www.dustinneece.com

Ordering Information: If you are interested in quantity sales for your organization, please contact Laurel Holland at laurelhollandh@gmail.com.

Wild Ginger Press
www.wildgingerpress.com

To my teachers and my students
who inspired this writing.

ACKNOWLEDGMENTS

During the last twenty years, I have had the privilege of working with masterful teachers and clients/students who dedicated great time and energy to transforming and uplifting their inner worlds. Both giving and receiving information contained in this book brought the Inner Power Wheel to life in me. The powerful practices of the Inner Power Wheel bestowed both liberation and peace to my life. I owe much gratitude to both my teachers and my students for helping me grow as a teacher and healer.

There have been many people who cheered me on to write and create a book from my work. My dear friend Cynthia Reardon, my son Dustin Neece and my sister Dawn Jepson were steady voices of acknowledgment and affirmation, telling me that what I was writing was valuable. I am not sure if I would have kept at it had these particular people not encouraged my writing. And thank you Dustin for painting the beautiful image for the cover.

My husband David Hajek made our marriage and home life a stable place where I could write, edit and wonder about how far I would actually take my writing life. My heart fills with gratitude for our relationship and life together. It is true that with great love anything is possible.

Cassie and Ericka Neece encouraged me to follow my dreams and my heart, listening to my tale of taking this book from an idea to a piece of work to share publicly. They are amazing daughters and friends. And thank you Cassie for your patience and creativity as we put the words of the book into images like the Inner Power Wheel and wall cards. Your confidence in the process relaxed me.

My inner circle of women, which includes so many beautiful hearts, held my desire to publish in enthusiastic warmth whenever I spoke of it. All of this love and energy kept me working at the task of making this book a reality.

Writing a book is surely a spiritual growth practice. Being bold enough to make public what comes from your heart and soul is not for the faint of heart. My appreciation and admiration for inspirational writing and excellent literature has exponentially expanded after undertaking this experience and seeing it through to completion. I am grateful to the many writers who inspire me. Their published words motivate me to look inward, to heal and to share. If my book does this for others, it will have fulfilled its mission.

A final thank you to my clients at the clinic in Framingham Massachusetts where I became a proficient psychotherapist. There were clients who told me I should write a book because how I helped them was so potent, so different. They planted a seed. Courageous Woman, Live Your Inner Power became the bloom.

ENGAGE YOUR INNER POWER WHEEL

and experience what you want

Do you want peace?
Peace resides within you, waiting for you to embody it.

Do you want joy?
Discover how to align yourself for joyful energy
and experience joy upon demand.

Do you want happiness?
Discover how to create happiness through living and
choosing consciously.

Do you want success?
Define success and then you will find your path to it.

Do you want to know yourself?
Discover within all the knowledge and wisdom that exemplifies you.

Do you want to understand life?
Life is waiting for you to discover and understand it –
you decide the limit.

Do you want normalcy?
You will create a new 'normal.'

Do you want freedom?
You alone can set yourself free.

Welcome to *Courageous Woman, Live Your Inner Power!*

CONTENTS

The Inner Power Wheel

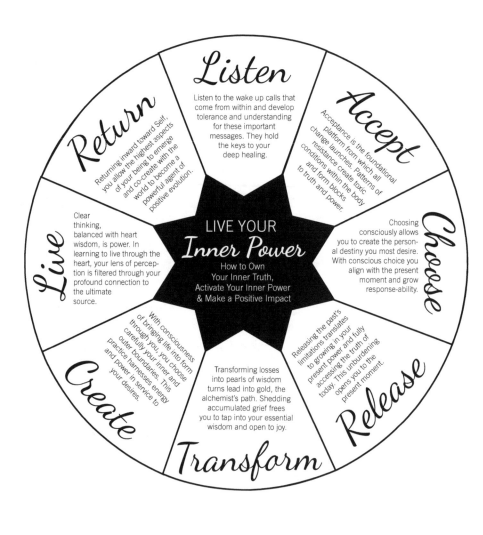

Listen
Listen to the wake up calls that come from within and develop tolerance and understanding for these important messages. They hold the keys to your deep healing.

Return
Returning inward toward Self, you allow the highest aspects of your being to emerge and co-create with the world to become a powerful agent of positive evolution.

Accept
Acceptance is the foundational platform from which all change launches. Patterns of resistance create toxic conditions within the body and form blocks to truth and power.

Live
Clear thinking, balanced with heart wisdom, is power. In learning to live through the heart, your lens of perception is filtered through your profound connection to the ultimate source.

Choose
Choosing consciously allows you to create the personal destiny you most desire. With conscious choice you align with the present moment and grow response-ability.

LIVE YOUR Inner Power
How to Own Your Inner Truth, Activate Your Inner Power & Make a Positive Impact

Create
With consciousness of bringing life into form through you, you choose carefully your inner and outer boundaries. This practice harnesses energy and power in service to your desires.

Release
Releasing the past's limitations translates to growing in your present power and fully accessing the truth of today. This unburdening opens you to the present moment.

Transform
Transforming losses into pearls of wisdom turns lead into gold, the alchemist's path. Shedding accumulated grief frees you to tap into your essential wisdom and open to joy.

INTRODUCTION

*The more deeply we move into our human consciousness,
discovering the power that resides within us, we rediscover
the truth that we are ultimately responsible for the
experience of life as we know it right now.*

W hat if you had the power to create the life you deeply want? Would you get down to the business of making your dreams come true? If so, you are reading the right book. You have the power within to create any experience you want; we all do. Your inner power may be latent because you have not been taught how to activate it in service to your best life. *Courageous Woman, Live Your Inner Power*, will equip you to work consistently with your inner world to achieve anything you put your mind to, especially when your heart endorses that desire.

Many years ago, I was not a courageous woman. By the time I turned thirty, my life looked quite nice on the outside: I was married, with two young children, living in a lovely home in picturesque New England. But on the inside, my world was a jumble of distress for a number of reasons. First, I had carried around a lingering burden of sadness since childhood that played out as a low-level depression. Second, while I had chosen well in 'dating' terms with my husband, he was not the love of my life, nor was our relationship the deep and passionate one I had always dreamed of experiencing. Third, I loved being a stay-at-home mom with my little ones, but was restless inside because I felt my marriage was a lie. That sense of dishonesty was pervasive because I imagined everyone looked at me and saw the American dream life fulfilled. But I wasn't happy in the most important way; I wasn't happy with me.

Because I greatly value honesty, keeping secret my distress concerning my marriage was causing depression – and I had no idea what to do. I had withheld my real feelings so long I wasn't even sure what they were, and because I wouldn't let myself consider my marriage a mistake, I couldn't acknowledge my deeper truth. Not having shared my distress with friends and family, I felt like a fraud. I was trapped in my own conflicted reality.

Are you living your own conflicted reality? Many of us are. When this happens, we live lives we don't feel good about. We are in relationships that are not fulfilling. We feel stagnant, unproductive; we are unhappy at work. We have feelings we don't like, and don't know what to do with; we feel unable to make positive change. *Courageous Woman, Live Your Inner Power* will help you address these problems and the inner distress that accompanies them by working directly with your inner reality. By activating the Inner Power wheel in your life, you can transform your inner world from distress and confusion to peace and clarity, bringing order to your outer life. The transformation happens *within you*, and is reflected on the outside. These lessons allowed me to transform my life and create my experiences from the inside out.

I didn't know I was discovering a sacred inner space when I started facing my distress, but once I began the journey of truth there was no stopping me. I made a commitment to clean up my inner home and create a sanctuary within where I could rest. Now I consistently turn to this inner world for guidance and wisdom.

My journey included a 25-year daily meditation and contemplation practice; returning to school for a graduate degree in counseling psychology; studying energy medicine in various forms; and teaching the ancient art of Tai Chi for 15 years, as well as meditation and stress management classes. I have grown a practice as a life coach, holistically sharing and teaching what I know about wellness and living a passionate life. Paralleling that inner journey, my personal life transformed through divorce; raising three children; learning to live without a 'significant other relationship' as I focused on other areas of life development; and eventually marrying into a union of passion and deep commitment to truth. My present excitement has been writing this book and growing a thriving business in the personal development industry.

The world is changing rapidly. We need the Inner Power wheel of action now more than ever to deal with the inner unrest caused by our attempts to manage the changes in the world without the necessary skills. We need new skills and new thinking to transform our lives in tandem with the fast pace of change in the world at large. Adopting a system to help you work with your inner world when you feel chaotic or lost enables you to move forward in new and creative ways. Through using the wheel, you move from reacting to life to responding to the world around you. It takes great courage to meet the level of change the world is calling for.

Courageous Woman, Live Your Inner Power is not a quick-fix handbook. The process described in this text is thorough, and intended to grow into a way of life. My goal is to connect you with the inner guidance system that will take you to whatever life experience you deeply desire. And you will fulfill dream after dream, because life calls on us to want more, to experience more, and to sense the great potential within. This book is for the marathoners of inner life, for those who are here to explore the inner world as the amazing frontier of adventure and truth that it is. I hope you are one of these inner explorers!

The practices of *Courageous Woman, Live Your Inner Power* create a medicine wheel – I love this concept of a moving wheel that heals and liberates. Once the wheel is activated, turning endlessly in your life, you experience health, wholeness and fulfillment. It also brings you face-to-face with what is discordant and unwell within, so that you may bring harmony and vibrancy to your life.

As you read through each practice you will come to understand its importance, learning how to use it to change, grow, and create wholeness within. A guided meditation helps you open to each practice for greater growth and understanding; journal inventories and inner power practices motivate you to dive deeply into the process. As you use the practices and reflect on your life through the lens of this medicine wheel, you will come home to your inner world where lasting wholeness is found. Through this emerging sense of wholeness, your ability to create the life you deeply desire takes hold. You discover as you put the actions into practice that you can indeed create powerful change inside, change that translates to growth and movement on the outside. Committing to using the medicine wheel will produce inner peace, as you clear away the inner debris and embrace living consciously.

This book is not a quick answer to things like how to find the partner of your dreams or how to find your true calling. Instead, you are guided into practices that will allow you to come into proper alignment with your inner life. It is here you find the aspects of yourself that know what you want, what you need and what feels fulfilling, joyful, exciting – you name it! When you are in connection to, and in alignment with, your deep inner truth, it becomes more apparent how to take actions that will bring about the aspects of life you have not yet experienced, but that your being yearns for.

What you are experiencing now in your life is a result of what you have experienced so far. Past conditioning leads to the actions you take every day and the choices you make moment-to-moment. Until you become aware of this truth, you will remain limited by that conditioning. The goal of *Courageous Woman, Live Your Inner Power* is to guide you in a process of reconditioning: by living consciously in the now, you can choose to stop unconsciously playing out old patterns that block your ability to achieve your desires.

The purpose of the *Inner Power* wheel is to demonstrate what is not working and *how it exists within you*. With that awareness you then open to doing it differently, based on *what you want*. The book is not going to give you the answers: it is going to lead you on an inner journey to connect with your own wisdom and insights. It then becomes imperative that you act on that personalized knowledge and intuition. You will be reconditioning yourself to live consciously in this moment where your power to choose exists, the power that drives your life where you want it to go.

What you can expect as you read this book is a close-up look at your inner life, a mirror held up to the real you, the inner you who is organizing your life. Dissatisfaction with any aspect of your life means you need to search your heart and mind for the root cause of the experience. If you are a little afraid to take a good look at your inner truth, you are not alone; many of the individuals I work with fear seeing what's really happening inside. To look at yourself – up-close and clear – takes great courage and determination. But until you learn that this is where your ultimate power resides, you will remain distanced from crafting the life you want.

Knowing there is darkness, distress, judging thoughts, or jealousy inside you simply means you are alive and fully human. We all have dark aspects; we all can be judgmental and experience negative feelings. It's how we respond to these aspects and act on this energy that shapes the truth of our experience. Ignoring them doesn't mean they don't exist or that you can't change them – only that you are 'choosing' to stay unconscious about these parts of your inner life. They are still organizing your life in a certain fashion. By not looking at these aspects directly, you lose the power to choose consciously and compassionately.

The process of change will vary for each reader based on what is happening in their inner world right now and what work is needed to create a path to your deeper wisdom and truth. Those who have been in counseling or have been on a spiritual path for a time may find the practices familiar. However, you will discover that the medicine wheel allows you to go more deeply inward and work more powerfully with whatever situation arises, both in your outer and your inner world. Those just beginning a healing path may find they need more help and support to dive inward and clear out the old conditioning. You may need to create a more effective support system to help move you into the quality of life you yearn for. *Courageous Woman, Live Your Inner Power* gives you a framework to consider how you have been conditioned thus far, and to acknowledge what you want to do differently going forward. It is meant to inspire you to sit still with yourself regularly, and in this stillness to discover the frontiers of your inner landscape where your destiny lies – to become the person you are itching to be.

There is no right way to read this book, though I encourage a slow approach and to have a journal beside you. You will want time to reflect on choices you have made, situations you find yourself in and experiences you want to examine in more detail, thus connecting with the power to choose more consciously. Once you develop this power, you will no longer recreate negative experiences; instead you will create experiences that bring joy and happiness. You will be forming the habits that elicit the quality of life you seek.

Reading the book once through and then returning to focus on each practice for a time is a useful approach. Taking at least a month for each practice, and considering how you put each healing action into your life daily is ultimately what is important. To become self-reliant and clear about what you want and how to go about it, practice and repetition are needed. As you develop awareness of your automatic and reactive behavior, you empower yourself to choose differently. Guided relaxation exercises in each chapter support you in creating habits that offer the time and space to understand your inner life in a new way. Your inner life becomes a sacred place of wisdom and guidance.

Consistency in practicing these exercises induces the most benefit; setting aside time daily for quiet and stillness establishes an inner habit whose value cannot be underestimated. You will condition yourself to connect with your own inner wisdom and intuitive guidance, clearing away whatever presently prevents your resting easily in this inner sanctuary. Additionally, spending quality time in this effort *when you are rested* means the greatest likelihood of increased insight. Finding a place in your home to be quiet, without interruption, demonstrates commitment that reaps great reward. Moving towards these conditions may take time, but progress results in heightened inner awareness, translating to growth and success. Before you begin the relaxation exercises, have your journal near enough to reach easily. You are encouraged to make notes about your experiences to increase your conscious awareness of the present moment and your inner world.

One of the myths about living consciously is that you will always be peaceful and serene; another is that once you 'become' intuitive, all is easy and clear going forward. This has not been my truth. I live consciously and spiritually awake; to me, this means challenging myself to grow, taking increasingly more responsibility for the quality of my days. It means facing myself in the mirror when I am not behaving with the highest integrity. I can allow myself to feel disappointment in my behavior, but come back into forgiveness quickly, make a course correction if needed, and continue to live consciously and boldly.

Sometimes, my intuition speaks and I still override it with reason – a forehead-slapping moment! Ugh – why didn't I listen? Recognizing how life may have been better had I honored that little voice within, I use that to fuel my commitment to trust my inner experience. I am content that life has its ups and downs; that nothing is perfect and everything is evolving perfectly. I live with feeling *simply human*, accepting that I am always learning and growing. I forgive myself, and others, regularly and compassionately when we fall short. I keep an eye open always to do my best, and in so doing, my life is good – very, very good. I rest easy as my outer experience aligns with my inner life.

Are you ready to commit to yourself, to discover your inner power to experience what you really want? I hope you are. Through putting the medicine wheel of *Courageous Woman, Live Your Inner Power* to action in my life, *I now see that only I am stopping my dreams, wishes and desires from becoming reality.*

My past conditioning can still block my dreams if I am not completely and utterly honest with myself. The journey toward living vibrantly and passionately today has been an amazing path of deep healing. One of the benefits of living the wheel of *Courageous Woman, Live Your Inner Power* is fully engaging with life around me, feeling a flow to my life. This flow seems effortless, and yet simultaneously, the challenge to grow into my full potential arises naturally within. This kind of growth requires exceptional, concentrated effort. Untapped resources continue to be revealed as I say *yes* to what my inner life calls for from deep within. My life has transformed into an amazing adventure!

As my clients grow and flourish using the medicine wheel of practices contained in this book, I become so excited about the possibilities of what we all can contribute and experience, individually and collectively, here on Earth. I love watching women connect to their inner passion and creativity, discovering that life is here for them to find meaning, purpose and adventure! I hope this book brings about that kind of awareness for you, too. If so, my intention for *Courageous Woman, Live Your Inner Power* will be fulfilled, because together we will be more vibrantly awake and creating a more loving world in which to live. You will become consciously bold and take action to have what you want, and enjoy the experience of creating it. May your life become all you deeply desire and may this book be a path to that reality.

Let's move into the wheel and begin practicing.

The Inner Power Wheel

Listen

Listen to the wake up calls that come from within and develop tolerance and understanding for these important messages. They hold the keys to your deep healing.

Return

Accept

Live

Choose

Create

Release

Transform

LIVE YOUR *Inner Power*

ONE

Listen to the Wake-up Call

Practice 1: Listen

When you listen to what is happening in your inner life, the path to fulfillment of your needs and desires uncovers itself in due course, moving you beyond any difficulties and into a harmonious existence.

My big wake-up call

I will turn thirty next week. My life looks so good on the outside. Most people would say – and my family truly believes this – that I am living the perfect life: an adoring husband, two beautiful children, and a lovely home. I am the stay-at-home mom I want to be. My husband and I are taking ballroom dance lessons – what a great guy he is!

My sad and terrible secret is that I am not in love with my husband. I do love him. He is a good person – kind, understanding, respectful, thoughtful, so many good things – but we are not the perfect fit for one another. I want more than good; I want wonderful and fantastic and passionate. And I feel guilty for feeling this way. It is eating me alive and I haven't the slightest idea what to do.

My family and friends don't know about this. In some ways I feel I've made a big mess of my life. I can't imagine getting a divorce: that's for couples who are angry and miserable with each other. We aren't either of those things. I am sad often, probably slightly depressed, and I can be moody, but that's nothing new, I've always felt great sadness about life. But I function well and life rolls along. I have a problem with canker sores, as many as four simultaneously, on every side of my mouth. I couldn't read aloud to my daughter recently because they hurt so badly. No medical advice has helped with this problem. It doesn't make sense. Like the truth of my life.

My husband and I are at a private ballroom dance lesson. Our sweet dance teacher chats with us for a bit after the lesson. I don't know what prompts her, but she asks if I had a troubled relationship with my father. Tears spring to my eyes. Before we leave she gives me the name of a therapist in case I want to talk with someone.

A few days later I stand in my kitchen, crying. I think, *I sounded just like my mother when I spoke to my children just then.* I am crying in the kitchen, standing still, looking at my life and thinking, *it isn't like my mother's – it's so different.* But it is alike in some ways: I am not happy; I am frustrated; my marriage is causing me inner pain and I am doing nothing to address that. And in that moment I make a silent vow that I will not repeat her patterns, especially the ones I watched, causing both of us such distress! She seemed helpless to do anything about her unhappy marriage. I will not walk her path.

After three days of crying, I surrender and call the therapist. I see him once on my own and he suggests I invite my husband to join us for couples counseling. Before long, we are going to weekly Adult Children of Alcoholics meetings. We have started a healing journey.

This was my biggest wake-up call. My inner distress finally got the better of me as I cried and cried until I couldn't function as I needed to for my children. How long had I ignored the truth of my complicated feelings for my husband? Goodness, nearly our entire married life. How long had I struggled with my deep feelings of distress about my parents' marriage, about their financial concerns? I felt I had lived my whole life with this heaviness. How long had my body been trying to get my attention with those mouth sores? It seems so symbolic now; I had so much to say, so much to share, but it didn't come out of my mouth. Instead, the energy remained within, where it literally caused eruptions.

There were wake-up calls all along. My being knew something was not right in my world, but I didn't know what to do. I just didn't know what to do. Finally accepting the fact I needed some help, turned it around – not immediately, but over time. Having someone (the dance teacher) reach out at the right time was a sign that things could be different; holding a mirror up to myself that day and seeing a deep, unacknowledged fear – of repeating my parents' patterns – was the first step to creating a new life. I'm so thankful that I responded to my wake-up call.

The call to be more of you

Collectively, we are on a life path that calls us to become more aware, evolved, and healed human beings. This process leads us to develop our creative nature. A natural part of this journey is outgrowing life experiences as we master them, giving rise to a desire to create anew. As a healthy adult, it is essential to identify when your life needs to be changed: wake-up calls come from within. They come from the greatest part of you, the part seeking more growth and self-expression. The courageous woman stays in close contact with the messages and signals emerging from her inner world, honoring and acknowledging them.

Listening to wake-up calls means meeting inner discomfort head on. You once had a strong connection to that inner call, the important guidance coming from within. If at any point you felt powerless to act on the voice's directions, this was good reason to disconnect from it. Feeling powerless doesn't feel good – and we all want to feel good; that's what motivates us to act. Remember how great it felt to master a new skill when you were young? That can continue throughout your life.

The call to become 'more' is considered natural in the early part of life.

New experiences are a natural rhythm of life: moving on to your next school becomes a rite of passage; changing friendships as you recognize who you are teaches you about beginning and ending relationships; finding recreational pursuits and a vocation that suits your desire to experience more and grow your personal competency structures much of early life. It feels natural to want to find out more about yourself and what you are good at, how you can contribute, and your place in the world. Wake-up calls are part of a natural growing process.

You want to learn how to 'do' life well. You want to make sense of your surroundings, the little world you live in and the big world out *there*. You want to feel good inside. All of this happens when life is going well and you are excited to be part of it. These wants and desires don't change when you age, but you may find you are not honoring your inner wants and desires. You may feel stuck in a life that somehow doesn't seem 'right.'

Growth is a natural part of being alive; growth experiences bring true fulfillment. Wake-up calls arrive when you sense that you need to grow more but don't know how – you're stuck. Sometimes the wake-up call is an intimidating call to action. You may want to turn away from it, fearing you cannot meet the challenge. Maybe you don't know what to do. The wake-up call wants you to BE more, but what?

The wake-up call asks you to make sense of why your life experience doesn't seem to fit with your sense of self. Somewhere inside, you have a sensor that compares your outer life to your inner world. Your outer life is a physical representation of your thoughts about the world, and who you think you are: what you want and need, and your beliefs about how to live. You choose mates and friends who reflect back to you your state of inner truth. You choose work you think demonstrates your personal and professional competencies. When you attempt to understand why you are living in a situation that doesn't feel good or 'right,' life seems more complicated.

Journal Inventory #1

What in your outer life feels out of alignment with your inner life? Consider your work, your important relationships, how you spend your leisure time and how you spend your alone time. Take time to imagine each aspect of your life and sense what feels really good and an authentic expression of who you are and what does not. Write about what is consistent with the authentic you and write about the inconsistencies. Are there any changes you want to move toward right away?

I can see – in the case of nearly every client I have ever worked with, and in my own personal experience – that we create our life situations to survive. Surviving is the primary human drive until we know we can and will survive. As long as you have breath, you will indeed survive. When you can fully provide for yourself, when you feel healthy and strong, when you feel capable and independent, when you feel fiscally sound, and when you feel curious and stable, you move out of survival mode and into thriving mode. When life is going well, surviving becomes second nature. Once survival is mastered, something inside seems to ask, 'is this all there is to life?' This question represents the larger You wanting more from life, getting ready to move from surviving to thriving.

Journal Inventory #2

In what area(s) of your life do you feel you are in survival mode? What areas bring up a sense of 'not quite enough,' a feeling of lack, or constant low-grade worry about whether it will be okay?

In what areas of your life are you thriving? As you think about these aspects, write about the qualities they bring out in you and what you most enjoy about them. This is important information about your innate talents and abilities.

Are there any changes that you know you want to make even if you don't know how to go about it right now? Journal about these.

Thriving and more than the ego

The call to become more of you elicits a deeper connection with your essence. You grow to want more than your ego is seeking. You shift from ego-oriented awareness into a more highly developed and evolved sense of Self. Experiencing the world from the ego alone causes anxiety, a feeling of heaviness, which grows burdensome. In short, we feel lousy and kind of empty. When we shift to a connection with a higher sense of Self – our soul/spirit – we feel light, expansive and curious.

The ego plays an integral, important role in our ability to grow. It is part of our mind, a part of our being that protects and supports us as we develop our personality and character. When the ego is threatened, survival mode takes over spontaneously. If you perceive a threat, you start to filter every choice through the need to survive. This means that your vision of the world, through the ego, can freeze in the belief that the world is not safe and you must work continually at survival. When you can look at your life and see that you are not in a life-threatening situation *and* you are still not satisfied with your daily experience, your Self may be calling you to more.

Inner Power Practice #1:

....

From Survival to Curiosity

Pose these questions on a regular basis to bring yourself fully into your power in the moment.

- Am I doing this because I want to or because I am supposed to?
- What would happen if I changed my mind and did this differently?
- Who told me this is the way I am supposed to live?
- Have I experimented and tried doing things differently when I feel unhappy?
- Am I looking to others for direction about how to live and the choices I am making?

When you look at your life through the inner eye of your deeper Self, it may look different than your conditioned perception. For instance, most of us were conditioned to believe that, as an adult, we would feel prepared to deal with life. If you look at your life from deep inside, and you don't really feel prepared to manage what you have going on around and within you, the perception doesn't match the belief. This mismatch usually elicits discomfort and stress, but not necessarily a solution.

When your experience doesn't reflect your beliefs about life and who you are, that Self peering out from within becomes restless, wanting to create a different situation. Something feels confusing, out of sync – life feels wrong somehow. This sense that something is not right can happen in many ways: perhaps words or phrases exclaim that something is wrong; certain feelings that make you uncomfortable, while nothing you do or say makes them go away. There can be a persistent vision of a different life that seems to carry some kind of coded message. The inner eye knows, can never *not* know, that life is out of order because it belongs to the big Self that helps you move forward, grow and change circumstances as needed.

This inner eye, inner voice and inner knowing all connect with your soul, the more highly evolved sense of self that wants your highest good, the good of those around you, and ultimately the good of all life. From this perch within, you can gain clarity on how to create a fulfilling and meaningful life. But first you must listen to its call to 'wake up!' – to get your ego in line with its greater vision. It is your choice to listen or to remain uncomfortable in your own skin.

Journal Inventory #3

....

What is the great vision of your life? Consider the big dreams you have had. Write in an unedited fashion about your dreams, hopes and fantasies of a wonderful life, meaning don't let anything stop you writing no matter what comes up in your mind. Let yourself express feelings, thoughts, images, as they arise. You may draw, tell stories, or simply write your stream of consciousness – the idea is to let it flow without holding back.

How the wake-up call arrives in your life

The wake-up call comes in infinite ways. Since we are all endowed with the beautiful gift of a big Self or soul, the call will be a voice that you recognize, but often wish to ignore. It will challenge you to be brutally honest about your life, and brutally honest with others. It will urge you to find the most meaningful and fulfilling experiences, experiences that may require the risk of letting go of the known. It may require entering territory that feels scary. Answering the wake-up call means liberation from the discomfort of living out of sync with your inner knowing and being.

Your particular wake-up call is unique to you: it may be a depressed mood; sadness about life being so meaningless; or a deep lack of interest in your current life. It might manifest as relentless discomfort with your body, over-eating, under-eating, drinking to numb emotions, shopping from boredom, talking about nothing and feeling empty, gossiping and feeling vaguely guilty, turning on the TV or computer because you don't know what else to do. Perhaps it's the inability to sit still for an indefinite period of time, or simply not knowing what you love, what you are passionate about, what you want to do that will cause creative energy to flow.

The wake-up call arrives all the time; the question is, are you listening? Are you attending to your feelings, your thoughts, and your inner world; to the discomfort, the restlessness, or the empty or conflicted aspects of your life? Are you numbing yourself to any of the above? Perhaps life is good enough right now and you don't need more. Perhaps you don't feel the need to wake up to the 'more' within that awaits your connection. When you *need* to wake up, the call will become persistent and uncomfortable. If your being is satisfied with the status quo, all is well – or at least, well enough for now.

How to discern the wake-up call from other voices

We all have a variety of voices in our minds, typically a mixture of the voices that direct life for us from the outside. These voices include, but are not limited to: parental figures, family elders, teachers, religious leaders, friends, societal figures, political leaders, and any other voice of importance in your life. They carry a slew of messages and beliefs belonging to the culture and environments within which you grew into adulthood. These voices have shaped and molded your mind, your feelings, and your current vision of yourself, the way to earn money, ideas about family, and your decisions about how to build your life so far.

Journal Inventory #4

Which voices in your head are vying to influence your decisions about your life? Who are the primary players from your past whose voices are still in your mind, calling the shots?

Make a list of them, describing how these individuals impacted your life, and what messages you received from them about how to live. Then go back and take inventory of your feelings about each person and your relationship with them now.

The voice of the wake-up call pushes back against these voices in some way; it wants you to think and feel for yourself. It wants you to discover there is more to life than these voices have taught you. Though the inner voice is quiet and persistent, it becomes louder and clearer once you give it some attention. Although responding to the call may seem to threaten the stability of your present way of life, it truly has your best interest at heart because it knows you on the deepest level. None of the other voices knows you as well as this one that calls for a greater expression of your Self.

The blessings of a wake-up call

Waking up to what is happening within you is the ultimate path to fulfillment. Given the cultural habit of directing attention outside of Self, listening within can be challenging. But everything that feels out of order in your life can be altered for the better if you pay attention consistently to the energy moving within you.

Doing this can seem overwhelming at the beginning when you may not believe you have the strength or skill to navigate your inner world; just trust the process described here. Finding the right support for this endeavor is essential, and will bring about forward movement in leaps and bounds. You will feel successful even though you may wonder where it all leads. Learning how to find healthy support is a life-long art. As you grow, your needs and strengths evolve: therefore, the quality of support needed also changes – this is natural. Beginning and ending relationships is a skill that grows with time and practice, but this art is imperative for a fulfilling life. With the right support, waking up becomes a natural, ongoing process.

Maybe you are asking questions about this process of waking up and listening to your wake up calls. Questions like:

- What does it mean to wake up?
- What does it look like to be vividly conscious to life?
- How will life change if I wake up fully?
- When is the right time to begin to change?
- What if I change my life and still I'm not happy?
- How do I know what I desire is even possible?
- Am I afraid of the work it will take to change my life?
- Isn't it too late for me to change some things?
- I made my bed; don't I have to sleep in it?
- What if I don't know what I want or what is wrong?
- What will everyone think of me if I start to act differently?
- What if my family/spouse/friend rejects me for wanting different things?

All of these questions represent resistance to your wake-up call. The resistance will come; you must persist regardless.

The truth is *now is the right time* to listen to the voice asking these questions or speaking these thoughts. You are *always on the path* that can lead to what you deeply desire. *Every moment is an opportunity* to follow the path to fulfillment. You discover a place of change and inner peace by committing to these things: to listen inwardly, be true to yourself, and act on behalf of what is deeply important to you.

Whatever you are doing, stop right now and respond to your wake-up call. Your habitual distractions are not always conscious, so it is imperative to take any small action towards the call. The call often comes as pain, confusion, or unhappiness of some kind, especially at the beginning. Listen to these feelings about your life; by moving towards them and seeking positive resolution, you make change happen. You become the creator of the life you want.

Inner Power Practice #2

Be on the look-out for habitual distractions. Pose these questions to help you discover what keeps you from living the life you desire:

What activities distract you from doing what you really want to do?

What activities do you do automatically without considering whether they have meaning or value to you?

Keep a daily record for a week of how you spend your time, hour to hour. After a week, categorize your activities and determine what feels like 'wasted' time.

Experiencing challenges in the process of change and creation are natural. It takes time to develop clarity of intention and then take persistent actions towards what you want. You may find others resist your need for change, which is why it's important to begin your journey inward. Only you have the right answers; as you act on them, you will feel better and stronger. You will experience new honesty in your relationships. You will sense an integrity that was missing in the past.

You will feel an inner calm arise. All of these things will happen as you consciously choose to respond to your wake-up call.

Open to your questioning, to your unrest. Let these feelings guide you inwardly, for beyond them, important information awaits. No one can tell you when you have the right answer or if you are on the right path: that knowledge comes from inside you. The inner journey is about becoming physically, emotionally, mentally and spiritually attuned to receiving and acting on your unique inner wisdom. Your inner wisdom wants you to grow, flourish and prosper, but it takes time and support to develop trust in it. Proper support will encourage you to discover more inner resources and to connect with the best outer resources to achieve your desires.

As you begin listening to your inner voice of wisdom – discerning it from the noise of the past, the draw of bad habits, the voices of resistance, voices of old teachers who lived by different values, and the conditioning that no longer serves you – it will become clearer and stronger. You learn to quiet the noise that overrides your inner voice of wisdom as you attend to your inner unrest.

Paying quality attention to your inner wisdom begins with mastering the next practice of the Inner Power Wheel – Practice Acceptance. When you listen inwardly and feel your inner discomfort, the desire to move away, ignore or deny this unpleasantness can be strong. Practicing acceptance is the next foundation-stone of a life of conscious presence, and of honoring your inner experience no matter how troubling it may seem right now. It is your next step towards inner freedom and resolution. Let's delve into the practice of acceptance.

Guided relaxation exercise for listening to the wake-up call

Take a few deep breaths and focus your attention on anything that calls your attention presently, particularly any inner unrest or discomfort. Allow yourself to stay with the feelings and thoughts. Breathe into them and let them all be there as fully as you can tolerate in this moment. Name the feeling(s) as accurately as you can. Notice the thoughts and what they may be asking of you.

Lie down if you can. Bring your attention to your breath. Practice relaxed breathing for a few inhales and exhales. Scan your body slowly, working your way from head to toes, searching for any tension. As you scan, notice the place that feels most tense and keep your attention focused on it. Now imagine yourself breathing gently into that place of tension, exhaling the tightness with every breath you release. Sense yourself calming and relaxing that part of your body for at least ten breaths.

Return to sitting position. Refocus on your breath. Let yourself relax and notice how you feel. Sit quietly and recognize the predominant thoughts that surface spontaneously. Stay with the thoughts briefly. Become aware of how your mind attempts to engage you in any thought at all, pulling you into a mental story and away from your breath. Just notice and keep returning attention to your breath.

Transfer your attention to your heart. Be as still as you can be. Ask yourself, what do I want right now? Stay focused on your heart and see what answer emerges. Give yourself some time. Do not hurry this process; do not necessarily accept the first answer as the final one. When you are ready, take three more deep breaths and slowly open your eyes.

Notice how you feel, paying particular attention to any changes since you began to relax. Make notes about each part of your experience, anything you recall. What was your predominant feeling when you began? Where was the place of tension in your body? What thoughts did you notice? What do you want right now? How do you feel after the exercise? Are additional thoughts, feelings, or desires emerging? If so, make note of them.

Repeat this exercise daily. Spend at least five minutes on it at first, and increase the time as feels right until you are spending twenty minutes or more on the process. This exercise is helpful at any time of day, but doing it morning and evening can be most beneficial.

The Inner Power Wheel

Listen

Accept

Acceptance is the foundational platform from which all change launches. Patterns of resistance create toxic conditions within the body and form blocks to truth and power.

Return

Choose

Live

LIVE YOUR
Inner Power
How to Own
Your Inner Truth,
Activate Your Inner Power
& Make a Positive Impact

Create

Release

Transform

TWO

Practice Acceptance

Practice 2: Accept

When you accept the totality of your experience in the present moment, you enter the true expression of your life; you grow in wisdom through a deeper understanding of your life thus far; and you open the door to creating life anew.

My story

Four years later, we have had a third child – another daughter – who is a delight and adds to the picture of perfection. I have experienced so much healing in the four years since my big wake-up call. The couples' counselor did what he could to get my husband and me functioning well, and communicating better. Our family histories of dysfunction related to alcohol use have been explored and addressed, producing much healing and relief. I have stopped many of my co-dependent behaviors.

During this time of change, I learn to practice acceptance in many ways as I reflect on my early life. I learn to accept my parents' choices, and to accept my siblings' choices as they also struggle with alcohol use. I learn that I cannot save anyone except myself. I accept that I developed some bad habits of people-pleasing as a way to manage my feelings while

I grew up. I accept that I don't speak easily, readily or well about my complicated, emotional inner world, but I want to be honest and must work to be forthright instead of withholding. I work on acceptance all the time, which helps me relax internally. My role now is to set the best and healthiest example I can for *my* children.

I accept that I ignored important feelings of disappointment and rejection early in my marriage when I was unable to express myself, not knowing how to get my needs met. It has been such a journey of acceptance and I have grown so much! Yet I still keep the big secret hidden: I am not in love with my husband. I want to be in love with him. I appreciate him and enjoy what we do have. I try so hard to be good, to be kind, and to be the best mother I can be. I want so badly to make this marriage work because I'm afraid of what it means if I don't. I still can't imagine divorce.

At a high school reunion, I feel a sudden strong attraction to my first love, an attraction that wakes up the passionate me who wanted great Love and Romance in her life. As I look again in the mirror, I receive another wake-up call. I see myself being dishonest and selfish in ways I have never acknowledged because I did not want to see this side of myself. I have actually 'used' my husband to avoid dealing with my complete truth. Never consciously, never intentionally, never maliciously, but I have used our marriage and his willingness to stay with me because I couldn't be honest about my journey of love with him. I couldn't say, 'I fell out of love with you very early on in our marriage. I see how we don't fit together. I am this passionate romantic who needs ALL of herself in this relationship – and a part of me left many years ago.

'You didn't see her go, you didn't call her back and you don't know her at all. I hardly even know her because she has been hidden for so long. I need her if I am to live my full, true life. For her to be present, I must leave this marriage. I know I cannot love you the way you deserve; even if you are satisfied, I feel like a fraud. And I keep putting this guilt on myself every day that I betray you by withholding this truth. I know

I can love more and bigger than this; that I have an untapped passion that wants to come forth and I need to experience this part of me.'

I had withheld all that because it was selfish, and I saw myself as better than that. I saw myself as someone who made a commitment and kept it; who made her bed and slept in it; someone who was true to her family and loyal. But I was none of these things to the real me and I had to accept this bitter truth. If I was betraying myself, then I was betraying everyone. Having accepted that, I had to figure out what was next. Practicing acceptance rose to new heights in my world.

Look around your life and learn not to judge

Acceptance begins within. Listening to the wake-up call conditions you to lean into acceptance more readily and reverse conditioning that has kept you unconscious to what is happening internally. Our internal world holds the key to our inner wisdom and the life we deeply desire.

Through practicing acceptance you open to the medicine – the knowledge and guidance – within you, which leads naturally to actions that will bring about peace and joy. Your truth is a beacon that guides you forward into a life of creativity, peace and joy. The life you are living right now is perfect for you in the sense that it contains the seeds of all you need to move into a life of great love and joy – even if your life seems unfulfilling or boring. The unfulfilling and the boring are your personal guides out of this quality of life and on to something greater.

Journal Inventory #5

Begin practicing acceptance by taking inventory of where you are now. Start a journal that clearly states what your life is about and what you want to change. As you consider and acknowledge what is happening in your life, do not make judgments about it, just list and acknowledge. Do not make judgments about how you got to this place, just list and ac-knowledge. Keep it simple and keep it honest.

When you find yourself thinking, writing or talking about how you have failed – how the quality of your marriage, your job, your friendships, or your life is 'bad' in any way – withdraw the energy of judgment from the process. Notice your feelings and write or talk about them instead. 'I feel disappointed,' 'I feel sad,' 'I feel angry,' 'I feel afraid,' or 'I feel at a loss about what to do.' These statements help you acknowledge your inner truth, rather than making this a mental exercise in judging and evaluating, which won't contribute positively to moving forward or rallying the power you need to create anew.

Honoring your feelings connected with the quality of your present life begins the cycle of healing and powers you forward. It's important to grieve the losses associated with life's disappointments, so we can identify the 'how' of change; grieving well also helps us see what we want instead. Identifying this important knowledge – 'what' and 'how' – is part of the creation process that you learn by living your inner truth and growing onward from the current conditions of your life.

Being in a safe relationship where you can talk these details through can be truly enlightening. The quality of relationship is essential though: you must be with a neutral other who can allow your full truth without judgment – a particular someone and someplace that can hold all the details of your difficulty. This support person must invite you to connect inwardly to connect with your inner guidance and truth and develop these assets effectively; proficient counselors and coaches have mastered this skill.

Journal Inventory #6

....

List the individuals who play a significant role in your life at present. Choose a scale (for instance - 1 to 5, 1 being the ability to listen and talk without any judgment, 5 meaning they seem to always judge) and identify your level of confidence in each person's ability to withhold judgment. Consider how comfortable you feel sharing the 'real you' with these people on a regular basis. Be on the look-out for how often you hold back from saying what you really want to say or being who you want to be in their company. Just notice, without judging.

Looking at your life without judgment may take some time and practice. We are surrounded by systems that judge and evaluate continuously, so it feels baked into our minds. Your environments, just like mine, may have conditioned you to judge yourself and others and it requires determination and vigilant monitoring of the mind to eradicate the habit. Practice, as well as being surrounded by less judgmental people, will help you change.

Practice noticing thought patterns and feeling patterns

Your thoughts are the energy of creation. They are your inner word. Word is creation – the leading edge of the creative process. What you think, you become. You have been conditioned to think in a particular way that has shaped who you are today. Every choice you make is related to thoughts stemming from beliefs that reside within you as truths. Some of these beliefs are conscious and some are embedded deeply in your mind where it is difficult to access them. Difficult, but not impossible!

Practicing acceptance means noticing the automatic stream of thoughts and feelings that are moving and dancing within your being right now.

This dance and this energy show you how you created the life you are living. You must become conscious of the dance as it is your platform for change. When you pay attention, you see that your thoughts and feelings relate to 'what is' and 'what isn't.' The time you spend on 'what isn't' keeps you in the loop of where you are – and don't want to be.

To practice acceptance means placing more thought energy on what is working well in your life and withdrawing it from the parts that are not working well. This change causes you to feel light, expansive and powerful – capable of creating anything! When you focus on what is not working, you feel heavy and burdened. You feel powerless and incapable of change. Such feelings do not support the process of creating life anew. Therefore, refocusing on what is working becomes a critical factor in your ability to create and move forward.

Inner Power Practice #3

Notice recurring thoughts and feelings, and name them directly. Say, 'Oh, here is this pattern where I feel _____ when _____ happens. Now I notice that I am thinking these thoughts again: _____ .

Moving forward means letting go of what is not working (literally releasing it), and focusing on creating what you do want. Putting your focus on what is not working and constantly running it through your mind reinforces *not working* and affirms *not having*. This is not a power-filled practice.

The most effective way to manifest what you want is through creating the feeling within you of *what it feels like to already have it*. This changes your vibrational state and alters your present moment powerfully. Feeling the happiness it will bring you, even though you don't 'have' it yet, makes you a magnet for what you desire. Holding this uplifting emotional energy encourages your mind to find ideas, avenues and actions to bring about the conditions you deeply desire. Then it is time to experiment with those ideas! Taking the steps to implement change then alters your experience in reality after your imagination created it in your mind and being.

The movement, the experimentation, comes from inside and expresses through you. Many of us focus our energy and time on attempting to organize life from the outside, to control the world around us. In situations that don't feel right, we don't like or we want to change, reflecting on what is happening internally will reap enormous benefits. Remember, your choices created the life you are experiencing. Those choices came from your inner world; even if you think someone else made the choices, you allowed them to do so.

Your inner life shapes your outer life. To make the long-lasting, fruitful and fulfilling changes you desire requires inner work.

Here are some examples of how the inner world shapes the outer world:

1. **The desire to be happy.** You may be under the illusion that your outer world controls your happiness. Happiness is an energy that arises in your being because of your inner awareness of life. You can induce happiness anytime through your thoughts and your perceptive state. This is truth – *You* control your experience of happiness.

2. **The desire for fulfilling work.** If work life does not provide the meaning and fulfillment you seek through this avenue of self-expression, the inner work of identifying how you want to contribute will move you towards positive change in your outer life. You then find or create the work experience that offers the feeling you seek – but only *after* identifying the inner want.

3. **The desire for a loving partner or friends.** It feels good to receive love and wonderful to give love; the mutual experience is divine. Self-love must come first, which means learning supreme self-care

and giving good attention to your heart's desires. This inner process leads to intimate and loving relationships. Partners in a mutually loving relationship *know* they are both loving and lovable.

Taking inventory of your inner experience and practicing acceptance reveals how much influence you have over your inner state. This influence is infinite. Imagine the power you hold to bring about the changes you seek!

Inner Power Practice #4

....

When you notice a recurring negative thought pattern, consciously withdraw your mental energy. Refocus your attention on something positive and productive.

As you observe recurring negative thought patterns, determine if action is needed to release the thoughts. Sometimes it is necessary to make amends, set a new boundary or have a conversation in order to bring some thought patterns to rest. Journal as needed to consider what actions will help you let go mentally and stay focused on creating versus stagnating.

Resistance and acceptance: observing the difference

Practicing acceptance is crucial to change. When you sense discord, discomfort, disappointment or a desire to turn away from your current experience, developing an accepting attitude is essential. If looking inward elicits discomfort, this signals some important discovery that can dramatically alter your life. Discomfort often elicits resistance, because it's natural to want to be comfortable and feel good. Resistance to your present experience causes tension in the body and throughout the entire being.

Rather than turning away from these thoughts and feelings, resisting them and distracting yourself, look within. Building tolerance for your range of feelings lets them flow through you, rather than becoming trapped energy that causes imbalance and illness. As you build tolerance, you will see the thought patterns associated with feelings that arise automatically: these are your conditioned beliefs, and are often what cause stress and discord within you. Learning to watch these thoughts and feelings, rather than getting lost in their energy and story, helps reconnect you to your authentic power. As you take a more detached posture, emotions can provide guidance. Conditioned thoughts can be set aside and you can utilize your wiser, more mature mind to make decisions.

With feelings we don't like or that distress us, we judge them, want to disown them – we want to abandon them. The ability to observe feelings without judging grows with practice. Acceptance teaches us to use the vital energy of feelings for growth and understanding. When feelings seem intolerable, finding unbiased support for expressing and understanding them is essential.

Healthy parenting provides an important kind of support as you grow emotionally. You may not have received this kind of guidance and love. If you know you did not experience the kind of parenting that taught you how to express emotions like anger, sadness and fear in a direct manner, you might consider professional support during this period of emotional development. With proper support, you can stop resisting emotions, and instead, express them in a respectful, balanced way. Until you become a healthy adult, you will feel a victim of your own emotions, and often those around you will too.

With practice, you no longer need to resist *any* emotion that arises, but rather you identify it and use it to propel you toward what you desire and away from unwanted situations and people. With acceptance you direct emotional energy in productive ways. With resistance you physically tense up, and hold them in your body creating discomfort. As you open to accepting what is happening and moving within, you can intentionally dismantle any accumulated resistance to life and the resulting tension.

Inner Power Practice #5: Exploring Resistance

Explore your chronic resistance patterns by tuning in regularly to your breathing and your body. Notice any shallow breathing and quickly scan your body to sense where you are holding tension. Identify any recurring thought patterns connected with the experience, as in: 'I don't like…,' 'I don't want to…,' 'this isn't working…,' 'I can't stand…'

Notice your emotional state; see if you can name it clearly and just stay with that truth for a short time. You don't need to do anything; simply build tolerance for the experience, breathe, relax and let go. Journal later about it as you wish.

The accumulation of your past resistance/constriction was slow and unconscious, happening over the course of years, and often started before you were mature enough to be aware of it. This tension remains when you habitually distract yourself from your immediate inner experience and any unhappiness in your life. The unhappy, uncomfortable feelings become frozen in place through your unconscious constriction and tension. You hold the emotional energy in your very cells, creating a toxic condition.

The more attention you pay to your life, the more you become aware of levels of resistance. Your resistance shows up in repetitive thoughts like, *I don't want to go to work today* or *I hate this commute* or *Ugh, I have to go spend time with these people.* All these thoughts reflect resistance to engaging more positively in your life; they create an inner world that says, *I do not like my life.* This never feels comfortable, bringing resistance accompanied by unconscious tension in the body. Subsequently, the physical constriction may come and go depending on circumstances. When the unhappiness or unrest is chronic, the constant inner constriction can lead to illness.

You can reverse this automatic constricting process and thus regain control of your inner responses to life, which means increased influence over your entire life experience. The reversal begins with accepting your experience just as it is: looking at what is right in front of you and saying, 'Okay, I accept this.' Looking at what is within, you say, 'Okay, I accept this,' not as in 'this is okay and I will do nothing,' but rather, 'this is okay, and now what?' It is *all* okay – simply because it is. Once you accept the truth and reality of life, you are empowered to get to the business of change.

Once you discover the part you have played in reaching this place of dissatisfaction, the knowledge and insight gained allows you, consciously, to stop repeating patterns. Acceptance empowers you with truth and is the beginning of change – opening you to new possibilities.

Replacing resistance with acceptance is medicine for your physical being. You literally dismantle the chronic tension in your body and allow your energy to flow more fluidly; your being re-engages in its own self-healing, self-regulating process that was disrupted by the tension. Your power in restoring your inner wellness is immense; your conscious, accepting, and loving attention brings about harmonious inner conditions.

Breathing and acceptance

Breath work is one of your most powerful tools. Using your breath consciously allows you to energetically release what you have held on to with inner tension and constriction. Shallow breathing becomes a signal that you are shifting from a relaxed state to a fear-based reactive posture, into fight or flight mode. Through conscious breathing, you open fully to your inner, as well as outer experience so that you can make fully conscious choices. Let's look at the benefits of conscious breathing.

Breathing was the first action you took as you entered the world; it's the action related to having been created. As you grow and breathe, you become the creator of your life experience. Without "breath" you are unable to maintain your physical being. The more consciously you connect with your breathing, the more you become aware of how the quality of your breath affects the quality of your experience. A shallow breath reflects tension and concern; a deep breath reflects relaxation and peace. Practice using your breath to alter your state of consciousness and you will discover how it supports you in creating the quality of life you desire.

Deepening the breath allows you to shift from fight-or-flight mode into the relaxation response. In survival mode we rarely make conscious decisions or thoughtful plans: we make decisions through the lens of 'life or death,' and rarely do we account for our deeper wants and needs. We become reactive to life, because our being senses danger. Unfortunately, your history may have conditioned you to respond in this reactive way, but the breath is the most effective tool for changing that.

Sensing when you are in fight-or-flight mode becomes a natural process once you give good attention to your breath. Make it part of your daily routine to practice deep, relaxed breathing, giving it time and your full awareness; healthy habits develop with time and patience. Start with a few minutes each day, and connect consciously to your breathing pattern. Relax as you do so. This practice reverses the habit of shallow breathing that comes with the fight-or-flight state, and need not be stressful or uncomfortable – it simply requires patience. Commit to being your medicine and recovering connection to your inner power.

Inner Power Practice #6

Challenge yourself to make a habit of relaxed breathing. Write a sticky note, buy a bracelet, or paint 'Breathe' on a rock and keep it with you until checking in with your breathing becomes a habit. Consider taking a yoga, Tai Chi, Qi Gong, or meditation class to enhance your ability to tune in energetically and master self-directed breathing patterns. Your life will transform!

Resistance and its deeper meaning – the ego and the soul

You may discover that you resist the habit of sitting still and paying attention to your breathing or your inner experience for even five minutes a day. Resistance often represents the battle between the big Self and the ego. At some level, your ego wants to continue to make the choices and be in charge: it wants to control not only you but everything around you as well! Once you let go, and accept the truth that you cannot possibly control everything around you, a big sense of relief arises from the deep recesses of your being. This is your soul saying '*ah finally!*' A big weight lifts as you let go of the need to control life.

I know from personal experience, and from those who have learned to let the world around them be what it is, that focusing on *how* you interact with life, rather than on trying to change what is happening around you, equates to moving into a sense of inner power. At the beginning, it can feel strange and a bit disorienting. How you interact with those around you will also change, and so your relationships may undergo change, some of which may feel good, while some change may entail a sense of loss that must be grieved.

Remember to lean into the grief, into learning the skill of grieving well as you make your journey inward. There is such beauty in deep grief when we open to it fully. Yes, grief can be very painful; building tolerance for your grief brings the benefit of really knowing the depth of your heart and the fullness of your love. Their infinite depth may only be experienced through a connection to your Self, your soul; they are the gift of knowing your heart and the essence of who you really are, beyond your roles and relationships, beyond your profession and your family. This is about meeting the eternal You, the inner enduring Self that is changeless.

Allow resistance: don't fight it and cause more resistance. Learn to watch it arise, and explore how following the resistance path keeps your life small. Sit gently with the resistance, breathe into it, and explore what is behind it. Feel the fear of the unknown; the fear of being alone; the fear of loss – the fear of success! Simply watch the feelings of fear. Do not engage in any mental process, but watch the thoughts and breathe. Know that you are slowly building tolerance that will move you from the small life of the ego to the greater life of the soul.

As you grow more comfortable with acceptance, it is time to practice the next step on your journey to creating the life you deeply desire: choosing consciously. Acceptance builds the platform to launch into new choices, to find ways of creating your life anew, beginning with small steps. You may want to turn life upside down and make a big change right now! Let's explore what it means to choose consciously and how to grow proficient in the next practice.

Guided relaxation exercise for practicing acceptance

Sit in a comfortable position. Bring your attention to your breath. Take a few deep breaths. Scan your body for tension, taking time to relax and breathe into areas of tightness. Spend as much time as you need to do this, relaxing and enjoying the feeling.

Now think about something in your life that you do not like. Bring the issue clearly into your mind. Notice how your body feels as you give attention to this issue. Scan your physical body for any tension. Notice your emotional state. Refocus on this disliked issue, and simultaneously, attend to how your body feels. If you cannot hold both experiences in your awareness, switch back and forth for a few minutes. This grows your ability to be in your experience and observe it.

Now notice your emotional experience. What emotions are you feeling as you focus on this situation? Stay with those feelings for a few minutes and breathe with them. Notice if they change as you keep your attention with them. Now notice any thoughts; become aware of the story the thoughts are telling you. Once you are aware of the storyline, bring your attention back to your breath and your body. Breathe deeply for a minute or so.

Make notes about your experience. Name your feelings and thoughts. Recount the storyline that grips your mind. Record any physical sensations connected with this story and issue. Write down any repetitive lines you heard in your mind. Record the judgments and beliefs that came into awareness. Simply record what you became aware of. Breathe deeply and relax after you have sufficient notes.

Now take time to write how you want the situation or issue to change; state the actions you want to take or you wish others would take.

Close your eyes and bring your attention back to your breath. Bring your attention to your heart and relax into this part of your body. Repeat inwardly, 'I accept my life just as it is right now. I do what I can to create the life I desire. My life is changing as I practice acceptance.' Stay with your breathing and repeat these affirmations for as long as you desire and notice how you feel. When you are ready, open your eyes and make notes in your journal.

Work through this process repeatedly as you take inventory of your life. Spend time with those parts of your life you resist presently, allowing yourself time to build tolerance for looking at the experience in a curious way. Notice judgment as you inventory the situations, but do not focus there. Instead feel the feelings, name them and make note of them. Make note of grieving work to be done by acknowledging disappointments, hurts and losses and do not push yourself to experience it all at once. Be gentle with yourself. Take time to be thorough in this process but do not rush it. Allow yourself to build up the inner emotional muscles to observe and allow emotions, and learn to keep the energy moving.

Close by consciously thanking yourself for dedicating time to your inner work. Breathe deeply, relax, and feel gratitude for giving yourself this time and attention.

The Inner Power Wheel

THREE

Choose Consciously

Practice 3: Choose

When you choose your actions, words and habits in full awareness, you empower yourself with your greatest asset: moment-to-moment consciousness, knowing you have employed everything available to create your desired experience.

My story

My husband and I progress slowly and carefully through the process of separation and moving on. I am learning about choosing consciously in a very immediate way, careful that each statement I make is in integrity with my truth. I feel cautious but clear about the path forward. I know I need this separation to honor the part of me that I have betrayed for so long; I must be honest with my husband about my complicated feelings around needing more in a marriage. We have tried our very best at this one, but I could not force myself to fall back into love. No hurrying or pushing: I am choosing carefully because I do not want to hurt him or our children any more than I fear they will be by their parents making separate households. I am afraid, but boldly stepping forward into this unknown and frightening territory.

As I make my deliberate choices, I see why I've avoided this for so long. What am I going to do? How will I support myself? What about that other vow I made that I would never go back to the corporate world? What am I going to do for work? How will I navigate the territory of mothering in a new way? Never wanting to face these difficult questions, I had kept myself safe from the scary world of parenting outside a marriage. I can no longer escape them.

Choosing consciously means I recognize that for every choice there will be a consequence, an outcome. I have learned this well through my life: in choosing one path, I forgo others. The more consciously I acknowledge this, the more I feel empowered to make a choice in line with my truth. My goal is to not look back and say, what was I thinking – where was my heart? I now engage both my heart and my good thinking, by giving time and space to my feelings, to vent and share as needed, and then to let the energy pass. I think about my goals, both the long-term and the immediate, and communicate with those who are involved about their feelings and thoughts. If anything, I may be over-communicating! Sometimes it takes tipping the scale the other way to return to balance. I am learning.

As I make these new choices, I think about the decisions, made years ago, that brought me to this place. I acknowledge sadness at my inability to listen to the distress inside. I had not known how to share my truth, how to ask for help when I was in over my head with life. My natural inclination is never to reach out, but to retract. I need help and encouragement to lean toward another. I had to teach myself to stay steady, observe and sense, and then make a choice based on what was happening inside and outside myself; to honor both experiences is to flow with life more fully.

As my husband and I navigated the difficult choices about where to live, who would be where, who would take what possessions, when this would happen – so many choices – we began to chart an unexpected path for our family. Some people in town thought we were still married and together; they were confused by our behavior. We weren't angry, saying nasty things to or about each other. We honored the fact we still loved one another by behaving well and kindly, despite the need to make our lives more separate. We wanted to be good parents to the best of our ability, so keeping a family life in some modified condition became the priority. We were seen together at school functions and around town; our children's friends saw us still sharing meals together.

We just decided to do it our way and figure out what was best for our family collectively. This helped us feel good about what we chose and consistently respectful of our unique path.

When dating others entered the picture, some of the togetherness passed and we allowed those new experiences to move us forward more separately. We lived within walking distance of one another's home, so the children could walk back and forth, which made our daily choices simpler. I was finally learning how to live as a conscious family, making decisions together, the way I had wished for growing up. Ironically, it happened after we were no longer a family living under one roof.

I would often be brought back to my past when I made important decisions less consciously. I took time to review how all that came to pass, how I came to be so disconnected inwardly when I am such an emotional person. I spent much time grieving this lack of awareness, the inability to assert my truth, own my full experience and share it more readily. This reflection showed me how my early patterns conditioned me to act and choose in ways that made me feel safe: for me, this equated to remaining silent when it would have been better to speak. I had not learned how to communicate and share myself, well and honestly. My past seemed such a burden then.

My choices had become reactive to my situation, to my troubled inner life, rather than responsive to my *inner truth* and to acknowledging the fullness of my reality. I work on establishing a habit of choosing pro-actively and considerately.

Consider the choices that brought you to the present moment

As you work towards wholly accepting your life as it is, you become aware of the choices that brought you to this situation. Becoming courageous and powerful means choosing consciously: you take responsibility for every action, every word you speak, every thought, and every hope. Conscious choice creates happiness and peace, while you grow strong and determined, aligning your choices with the deepest and truest aspects of yourself. You hold immense power through personal choice.

By practicing acceptance and observing your experience, you can consider how your life became what it is. You may think you chose consciously, but upon closer examination you may see that you were/are stuck in a stream of routine action and rote, ongoing inner dialogue. Through the practice of acceptance, you can now consider these habitual choices carefully, realizing that it is possible to choose differently. You can change any pattern of routine, unconscious actions.

This stream of routine action often takes on the form of the cultural trance, where we automatically make choices that are unhealthy, unwise, and self-destructive. These choices are made without conscious attention to the full truth of what we are doing, because we see it going on around us. Overspending, over-eating and chronic television/screen watching are all examples of the cultural norms that are literally killing us. When you are living in the cultural trance, you do not question cultural norms: you are detached from how your individual actions contribute to the quality of your life and the world at large. You forget, even deny, that you are responsible for your life, as well as influencing the quality of others' lives. You abandon your inner power.

Recognizing reactivity through moment-to-moment observation and acceptance shows you where you have lost connection with your authentic inner power. Reactivity can be hard to discover, because you may be comfortable in the way you have been living even if you don't like it, relying on known patterns because you don't know what else to do.

These reactive patterns arrest your ability to move forward and become a creative force in your life. As you consciously create your life, experimenting with new ways of being and engaging, you manifest a journey that is truly your own, by choosing carefully and thoughtfully. This may sound both exciting and frightening!

Journal Inventory #7

Make an inventory and keep record of your reactive patterns. This is the first step in gaining power over them and regaining the ability to respond well. It is often difficult to do in the moment when it is happening, especially when you are emotionally embroiled in the experience. Be sure to take time regularly (daily is best) to reflect and record any reactive experience. It will look like this:

When _____ happened, I suddenly felt _____ and then I did this _____. This behavior led to this and then _____ happened. I couldn't stop myself from saying and doing _____.

The blanks may be quite involved!

To avoid becoming overwhelmed emotionally, move through this process of choosing consciously without haste. Review the choices you've made *without judgment*, realizing that you can make new choices to change the trajectory of your life, its quality, and content. Avoid a sense of urgency so as not to create a reactive situation that may bring more dissatisfaction and frustration.

You need not have answers to any big questions that arise in reviewing past choices; concerns will resolve themselves naturally in time. Change will evolve organically from within as your experience of acceptance and conscious choosing grows. Stick to smaller choices associated with your daily routine in the beginning; starting small reaps big rewards.

Choose differently or with awareness in the small ways

In considering how consciously you are steering your life course, begin by examining your life closely. Looking at your routine – daily, weekly, monthly, yearly – is essential practice for aligning thought, word, and deed. Aligning your stream of thought, the words you speak, and your daily actions with your inner truth is essential to becoming a conscious creator of your life, a life that is fulfilling and meaningful. Aligning thought, word and deed with your highest value system results in up-lifting not only your life, but the entire human race.

Begin by looking at small things you want to change, changes that push back against unhealthy cultural norms. These are simple examples of small change with big benefits.

1. Eat a healthy breakfast with protein content to start your brain and metabolism operating optimally.

2. Walk more.

3. Turn off the television at least an hour before bedtime or get rid of it altogether.

4. Sit quietly for at least five minutes daily.

5. Smile more often.

6. Listen without interrupting.

7. State aloud what you are grateful for every day.

8. Eat one more fruit or vegetable serving daily.

9. Take at least five minutes each day to reflect on the day's events.

Small changes are manageable and let you master new habits more readily. You will often find that something major begins to shift. Change doesn't have to feel traumatic or monumental or grueling; it can be gentle and empowering with consistency and dedication.

Conscious choice is acknowledging your power to create change in the present moment. This means bringing full attention to the moment and choosing carefully and wisely. Practice looking at what you do, and asking yourself consistently if it is from habit or choice. Asking trusted others for feedback can add to your expanding self-awareness. Practice looking at your life in its totality, determining what you want to change and what you want to hold steady for now. Keep this process alive through daily, weekly, monthly practice and review.

Inner Power Practice #7

Choose three small things you want to change as a way to gain conscious direction over your current life habits. Make them small, specific and attainable. Do them until they are new habits. Continue with three more.

Time spent in reflection will encourage motivation. What are you doing in a moment-to-moment way that is in line with what you say you want, who you are, and what you value? For example, if health is important to you, what actions do you take daily and weekly to care for your health? Your actions – including your thinking – reflect the truth of who you believe you are. When you examine your actions, you learn the true story about your life.

Inner Power Practice #8

Create reflection time daily. Sit with your journal and take inventory, post items of gratitude, or simply write whatever feels right. Start with five minutes daily. Expand the time to twenty minutes over the course of the next month or two. Reflection gives you the power to turn experience into wisdom; wisdom grows your inner power.

***

Move into the big choices with awareness, consciousness and inner power

Developing an awareness of repetitive, automatic thinking is the beginning of a powerful process of change. You can consciously redirect your thinking as you become more proficient at observing your thoughts, rather than being absorbed in them. Examining your thought process gives insight into how you are creating life through your thoughts. Remember, your word is your creative force, and your thoughts are the leading edge of your words. As you make this realization, you become connected with your inner power and how it operates in your life. You realize the importance of self-directed thinking, gaining confidence and momentum to choose consciously on a grander scale – perhaps making some long-desired, but frightening changes.

When your actions align with your true beliefs, your thoughts and your spoken words, you powerfully create what you desire. Redirecting your thinking to align with your deepest desires, while taking action toward them, generates the fuel to ignite the life you want.

Aligning Desires – Thoughts – Actions = Power for Creating Life

Consider how your actions tell a story about you. Looking at that story enables you to alter your choices in alignment with the life you say you really want. At times this means making difficult choices, perhaps disappointing others, or acknowledging a part of you that has been buried, but calls from deep within.

Choosing consciously means listening carefully to what is going on within you. It means taking complete responsibility for the quality of your life, exposing and exorcising any victim posture. This can be unnerving if you have found comfort in blaming your current life condition on someone or something else. Taking responsibility means you no longer blame others for your present life. You accept that you have the power to create life as you wish and you never again give others power over the quality of your life.

Journal Inventory #8

Make a three-column sheet with these headings:

Desires   Thoughts   Actions

Fill the sheet in daily as a way to begin to align your inner world in support of creating your outer world on a more consistent basis. Just noticing and encouraging the flow from inside to outside will create a shift in time.

Take responsibility for choices even when you are angry with others

Past events and resulting feelings of blame and anger are big stumbling blocks for many while developing the habit of choosing consciously. As you review past choices, it may be easy to see how you were influenced by others, how your parents may have fallen short of healthy and loving parenting, how someone hurt you very deeply, and how the world is hurting in many ways that create havoc in your individual world. These kinds of conditions often lead to feeling angry with people, events and circumstances of your past, at the world today or even at your higher power.

Anger allows you to identify what you want, what is important to you and how to organize your life to support the truth of who you are. We often don't know how to use anger as fuel for change because we are rarely conditioned to view anger this way; instead, we misdirect it towards others or hold it in, where it is toxic to our physiology. Tolerating anger, asking yourself to be clear and definite about what is causing the anger to arise, means beginning to use your anger wisely. Identifying what you want to do differently so that you are not in the anger loop empowers you to create positive change. Remaining in circumstances that are frustrating and unhealthy means you will also feel angry with yourself.

In order to move beyond anger, you must consciously choose to free yourself to the present by letting go of your past. You discover you can forgive and let go, you can make new choices today, and you can create cooperatively with those who have similar goals, values and intentions. Putting your inner power to best use means you make new choices that align with a positive and exciting life. The need to be burdened by an old story holds little interest when you live a life that feels good and true for you today.

Here are questions that are helpful to pose. Allow answers to arise from deep within, not hurrying or forcing the process.

1. What are my deepest values? (What is most important to me in this life?)

2. Which relationships in my life align with my values enough to continue them?

3. Who in my life drains my energy when I am around them?

4. What do I want from my work experience?

5. What excites me and causes passion to arise in me at the deepest level?

6. What small changes will support my personal growth and transformation?

7. What excuses might I be using to avoid taking action I really want to take?

8. If I only had one year left to live, what would I do with my time?

9. How do I give up my power to choose for myself? What do I gain from doing this?

Simply answer the questions and acknowledge your truth. If you are not aware of the answer immediately, continue to pose the questions gently and allow time for answers to arise. As you fully embrace your inner truth, it becomes easier to make choices in alignment with it.

Journal Inventory #9

Explore your personal patterns regarding how you behave when anger arises in you. Tune in to the quality of the anger: is it irritation, resentment, rage, frustration? Notice thoughts that come up. Check in with your body and notice the physical sensations related to the anger. Record your experience and your behaviors.

How might you authentically share your experience going forward without including behaviors that may be harming you or others? Developing the ability to talk about the experience without being reactive, aggressive, or withdrawing is powerful growth. Begin with your inventory and set intentions about how you want to change going forward.

Develop inner power through conscious choice

As you begin to choose consciously in alignment with your true values, you feel powerful! When you feel powerful enough to act well, you are living in tune with your inner authentic power. You make a strong statement about who you are through the life you live. As we all live in this manner, the world reflects those high qualities we all crave.

Your deepest nature embodies qualities such as love, beauty, truth, joy, efficiency, prosperity, and harmony; inner conflict arises when you live out of tune with this nature. As we collectively play out our inner conflicts, we observe outer conflict in the world: war, poverty, impatience and intolerance, misery and unhappiness manifest around us when we accept these inner conditions without seeking a harmonious and joyful resolution. This is why it is important to begin within the Self, for when we collectively take responsibility for our inner condition and align with our deepest nature, the world begins to heal at the deepest level. We collectively create conditions ripe for harmony and love.

Inner Power Practice #9

Identify your current top three high value/qualities. Use these words as mantras while you sit quietly for a few minutes. Repeat a phrase such as, 'I embody wisdom, truth and clarity' as you focus on your breathing and your heart. Journal about simple, small ways to express these values/qualities more in your daily life.

Choosing consciously makes you aware of how much power you have to create the quality of the world within and around you. Determine that you want love, beauty, truth, joy, efficiency, prosperity, and harmony, and your thoughts will create and express these qualities in your own life through your actions. You will feel authentically powerful and joyful. This is the positive loop of conscious choice that connects you with your inner power and grows courage to challenge yourself further.

As you continue considering the changes you desire, the past comes up for review. Making peace with the past and then releasing it attunes you to the present moment in the most powerful of ways: you let go of old beliefs that no longer fit the true you; you free yourself of inner heaviness that may burden you; and you more readily open your heart to what you want to create. Let's look at the process of releasing the past as our next practice on the Inner Power wheel.

Guided relaxation exercise for cultivating conscious choice

Sit in a comfortable position. Focus your attention on your breath. Take a few deep breaths and then scan your body for any tightness: breathe into the tightness and relax it as best you can for a few minutes.

Review your daily routine. If it is evening, review the day; if it is morning, review the previous day. Imagine yourself from the moment you awoke, remembering each experience as best you can. Slowly take yourself through your day and notice anything you wish you had done differently; make notes in your journal.

Close your eyes again and focus on your breathing. Relax your body and focus on your heart, directing the breath to this area. Take your mind back into the day's review. This time, imagine each experience happening in the way you wish it had, and yourself acting in the ways you would have liked. Notice how you feel as you make these changes. Return your attention to your heart and breathe deeply for a minute or so. Make notes in your journal as you finish your practice.

Develop an evening habit of reviewing your day in reverse chronology. This allows you to completely release the day and be free to step into the next day unencumbered by the previous day's energy. Do this without judgment or comment; simply recall every detail you can, rewinding the day like a movie playing in your mind. Breathe and release. Relax and let go.

Complete your relaxation experience with a phrase or affirmation about the life you are currently creating. Let this be a guiding statement: *I chose carefully throughout the day to become aligned with inner integrity and peace.*

The Inner Power Wheel

Listen

Accept

Choose

Release

Releasing the past's limitations translates to growing in your present power and fully accessing the truth of today. This unburdening opens you to the present moment.

Transform

Create

Live

Return

LIVE YOUR
Inner Power
How to Own
Your Inner Truth,
Activate Your Inner Power
& Make a Positive Impact

FOUR

Release the Past

Practice 4: Release

When you fully release the past, you unbind yourself from being driven unconsciously by history: instead, you open to the truth of the present day and the characteristics that aid you in creating the ultimate expression of yourself.

My story

I spent several years in psychotherapy telling my story and holding my truth up to the light. I practiced the ancient art of Tai Chi and meditated daily, connecting with my inner peace and deepest truth. Through this connection, I became capable of consciously choosing actions based on these inner resources. I spent many hours crying, mourning, forgiving and letting it all be; I worked the Medicine Wheel of the Shaman of the Andes; I learned about energy medicine and experienced many healing ceremonies. This deep healing work connected me to a community of like-minded folks who also wanted to live more authentic, peaceful and compassionate lives. The ceremonies taught me ways to honor the important new rules I was adopting that were in alignment with my authentic self. I tapped away (Emotional Freedom Technique) emotional energy that still disrupted my ability to open to the full potential of

Life's abundance. I filled journals, wrote my stories and spoke to many groups about my life. The past was a large and guiding force in my world. Now, I both honor it and rejoice in its dissolution as I shed my past's ability to create my future.

So how did I release my past? All the above techniques and practices demonstrate my work and my process. But mostly I attribute my release of the past to recognizing it as a hindrance to creating life freely and to its full potential. I realized that, in order to choose freely each day, I must search rigorously and consistently for any belief, thought or behavior that was motivated by old conditioning. That conditioning from my past had caused me to be a people-pleaser, to swallow my truth, and to hide my inner world. It made me do things I thought were 'right' according to other people's rules, to do the 'nice' thing rather than the honest thing, and to sacrifice my own strong belief so that I might appease someone else's feelings or avoid the possibility of hurting anyone. All these patterns meant I disowned my inner truth to avoid other people's reactions, which in turn meant they couldn't know the full truth of the situation. This behavior on my part co-created a lack of authenticity for everyone involved.

To change that pattern, I began with myself. I looked in the mirror to see the truth of my feelings and my deep, inner truth beyond what I thought I 'should' be doing, based on others' rules and what I had learned about the rules of life. I needed to look at each pattern as it happened and say, do I feel good about this behavior on my part? And if not, what feels right to me? I could then look at the behavior and ask myself, what life rule is associated with this pattern?

For instance, when I withheld my feelings about what I wanted, I asked, what am I really doing? Often, I was avoiding conflict – the conflict of other people potentially pushing back. I was avoiding other people sharing feelings in opposition to mine. I was avoiding feeling bad if I caused someone else to feel bad about his or her behavior. My unconscious life rule was, don't add problems and conflict through speaking your truth. Keep the peace at all costs.

Once I saw my behavior and identified the old rule, I could hold it up to the light and decide whether it was a rule I wanted to maintain. Was it in line with my value system, my sense of the highest good for all involved, and did this rule make sense given the situation? These are questions I posed to myself over and over, as I released my past to live more consciously in today. I let myself make new rules again and again, and I proudly owned them.

Some new rules, like letting conflict come into the light so that it can be handled compassionately and directly, took me some time to live with comfortably while I grew new skills. But because I passionately believed they served everyone's highest good, I committed time, energy and attention to making these changes.

Releasing the past allows me to live in the present moment with conscious awareness, to use my compassionate attention consistently as I remain connected to the now. As I sense into my full experience, I gain greater skill in letting the past serve me, instead of serving my past by sacrificing my present truth.

Old rulebooks and old stories

As your awareness of choosing consciously grows, you are transported on the journey of reviewing past choices, many of which you might consider mistakes or poor choices. When you more fully accept and understand these past choices, you transform your past into wisdom that guides you to choose more effectively going forward. The more conscious you become in your connection with your inner Self, the more you are able to discern when your choices are driven by the past, rather than your present desires. Without reviewing these choices and mourning the losses of the past, you miss opening to growth in significant ways.

Living your inner power feels exciting once you discern how your past rules your present. With this shift, your energy and attention are infused with all the possibilities of how you might create life today, rather than feeling limited by past experiences and unconscious rules.

You become aware of your inner authentic power *to choose in alignment with what you desire now,* because your choices are no longer defined by your history. Releasing the past means you are no longer defined by your mishaps or your successes, your victim stories or your good girl stories. Instead, you find an enduring sense of Self that weathers all storms and joys, accepts all of life, and lives wholly with everything within and around you.

In order to find the Self that weathers life more easily, a lingering past must be removed. At least half the time I spend with clients focuses on accepting the past for what it *was* and making peace with every aspect of it. With this peace, you are no longer bound to a past delivered to you by your family, your circumstances and the culture. You realize that the past exists only in your mind, that the old stories within you are shaping your present experience. Releasing your past gives you the freedom to create a life of your own choosing, not a life limited by *shoulds* and *musts,* those rules driven by fear or an outdated life rulebook.

Unconsciously perpetuating old rulebooks keeps us all living in a dark age of rules like, 'children should be seen and not heard' and 'do as I say, not as I do.' These damage our growth as aware and evolving human beings. We are developing new rules like, 'children live spontaneously and often tell the truth naturally, so it might be wise to consider what they are saying' and 'you see what I am doing, so if I want to be a good role model I'd best choose what I do consciously, since no one is being fooled.' Emerging new rulebooks acknowledge a deeper truth of living consciously, no longer relying on intimidation and 'power over' to control others.

Journal Inventory #10

Explore your old rulebook and write a new one!
Begin by identifying five to ten rules that you've been living

by for a long time; determine whether you want them as your life rules today. If not, rewrite any rule that feels out of alignment with your true belief and value system. Carry your rules around with you for a while and read them daily – a few times daily is best. Be sure that your rules are in integrity with who you are and how you live today. Notice where they don't feel congruent – really feel into them. Any incongruencies signal a need for new rules or changes in your life to reflect your 'authentic' Self. This should be an ongoing process until your life, its rules, and your being feel in alignment.

Example:
Old rule – To be accepted and liked, I need to be nice.

New rule – I need to be my authentic self, so that I attract and connect with friends who are a natural fit for me.

The old rulebooks are losing their usefulness as we outgrow the need to shape our behavior through fear. Instead of relying on fear of punishment, fear of retaliation and fear of judgment, we can choose to behave in kind and respectful ways because we believe in the goodness of those qualities. We live in the qualities of our deepest nature because we hold the highest good of all in our hearts. This can be hard to do if your heart is walled off from a past that taught you the world is not safe.

The world becomes a safe place when you know you can keep yourself safe inside. What I have learned and what I see with clients is this: past conditioning is perpetuated by **you**. For instance, if you believe yourself unworthy of the undivided and unconditional attention and love of others, because that is what you experienced growing up, you continue to accept marginal attention and love from others today. When you condition yourself to believe that you deserve loving, quality attention from others, you develop healthy connections with people who offer that.

You do it first by giving it to yourself and then asking it from others. It doesn't happen magically – you create the experience purposefully, largely by noticing how you perpetuate the old stories **through** you today. Then you choose to stop the thinking that leads to those behaviors.

Noticing your old stories becomes a new habit as you pay attention to your thoughts and behaviors. Listening to the words you use when you talk will give you clues to how you are living in old stories, rather than in the possibilities of today. You become more aware through practicing acceptance and considering your choices with full consciousness, tuning in when the old stories and limiting beliefs arise in your life today. You pause and decide to go forward in a new way. You realize you can choose differently, creating new patterns and habits that support your growth and your dreams, rather than continuing unhealthy, debilitating patterns.

Inner Power Practice #10

Notice when you are telling stories about the past. Identify story themes that you return to often. Simply noticing is the beginning of bringing needed closure to old stories.

Ready for release

You are ready to release the past when you see how it limits the positive quality of your life today. Just noticing the old stories – those old rules and beliefs that are not your deepest truth – starts you moving forward. Unfortunately, the past is literally woven into your being by your thoughts, feelings and behaviors, which makes releasing the old ways challenging.

I consider it a bit of a dance for a while as you slowly unwind yourself from your history. It is as if you are unpeeling an onion with many layers, seeking the innermost layer that is free to create in an unencumbered way. Often you make a change and then discover another limiting belief that needs altering, and behaviors attached to that belief that need altering. This process requires persistence and consistency. Although it can feel long and arduous at times, the release process also feels liberating and empowering.

Releasing the past is a journey filled with awe. Many surprises await you when you boldly search your history for its truths and the ways it shaped you. One of the most courageous aspects of owning your life as it is today is taking responsibility for how your history has guided you to this moment, and then consciously choosing whether those old patterns and beliefs fit the authentic you.

Sometimes this can be painful. When the journey is painful, often it holds great potential for liberation. Accessing the potential masked by your history, and unearthing the light that may be buried within you, leads to your truest and most fulfilling life.

If you choose, courageously, to search your history for a fuller understanding of your present, I recommend using the right support. Often your perspective is skewed by your history, and another's assistance helps you uncover the truth. The more emotional the journey, the greater is the need for support. The art of navigating life well independently, *or inter-dependently,* develops naturally as you feel more powerful in your authentic self. Just as a child needs assistance to grow into adulthood and independent living, you need support to grow yourself fully when you discover places inside that are particularly vulnerable. Asking for help is a wonderful skill to learn and use wisely.

Inner Power Practice #11

Begin to create your healing spaces and circles by identifying people in your life who can hold space for you without judgment.

If you know you need to talk about your past and need help with emotional expression and letting go, challenge yourself to find a counselor or coach.

Decide that you will make connections wherein you can authentically share your old stories and find closure.

The ego grips and the soul guides the release

Releasing your old story creates a new vulnerability in your life: you see how and where fear has shaped your life. You must be prepared to discover new aspects of yourself and to face your inner darkness. Your ego will take a bit of a beating along the way as you review choices that now seem unfortunate and self-defeating. It is important to know that your history serves you well when you *learn* from it. Sometimes you will feel an internal struggle, some resistance, or the desire to 'not bother' because your ego avoids learning – it believes it already knows everything! The ego will slow down your process in the following ways if you do not develop a proper relationship with it during this process.

The ego wants to be right. You must decide not to live in a right/wrong paradigm, but instead be accepting and open to what is, what happened and what you want as you go forward. You must want to create a positive life experience more than you want to be right. You must let go again and again in many ways, allowing yourself to leave the past in the past regardless of who did what.

The ego will back away when fear arises. The ego wants to look strong, brave and invulnerable. You, however, are in a vulnerable space during learning and growing – that's *how* you learn and grow. This can feel scary! You must come into the biggest part of yourself and remember that fear alone cannot harm you. Fear will only limit your ability to continue moving forward to realize your dreams. You must want to learn and grow more than you want to feel safe and secure in the known version of your life, the old story. Staying with the process when you most want to move out of it requires courage.

The ego will want to look 'good.' That means the ego will steer you away from making a mistake. Learning about life and finding out who you really are, then feeling the excitement and joy of expressing the authentic you in the world takes some trial and error. To navigate the process well, you must be willing to risk going down the wrong path to find out it doesn't feel right, make you happy, or fulfill you. You can always change your mind. Accepting you are on an adventure that may include mishaps as you learn and grow helps to move you out of the need to look 'good,' 'successful,' or any other label that the ego clings to.

The ego wants to look successful. The ego wants only to be successful. Refusing to define yourself by your successes frees you to step into new experiences and new beginnings. The wisdom gained from experience provides momentum if it allows for change, which may mean starting out as a novice as you learn a new proficiency. Sometimes you redefine yourself at unexpected moments: discovering new aspects of you un-tethered from the past makes further growth possible and joyful.

As the ego grips the past to define you, so that it can 'be right,' 'avoid fear,' 'look good' or 'appear successful,' you must rally the soulful aspect of your inner self to guide your journey forward. You must anchor to the places within that understand being right is an illusion, fear is the great enemy to be confronted directly, looking good is a mask, and that past success is history. Your soul must be willing to sacrifice the illusions of being right, safe, good, and successful for the excitement of discovering the real you, experiencing a life of purpose and meaning, joy and peace.

Journal Inventory #11

For the next week or two, review your days and notice:

- your ego wanting to be right

- your ego moving away from fear
- your ego wanting to look good
- your ego wanting to look successful

Write about what triggered those reactions in you.

The gifts of releasing

The gifts of releasing the past are life-enhancing on a daily basis. They include: living with excitement at the possibility of what you can create; finding meaning and a purpose that expresses the inner you; and living in lasting joy and peace.

Living in excitement at what you can create arises naturally as you free yourself from old burdens. Your creative energy can be blocked by old relationships that caused you harm and confinement, and still impact how you react to the world around you. Today's possibilities may be defined by the unconscious rules you adopted within your old relationships. When you release connections from the past, particularly those that caused you inner conflict, you unplug from a draining source; you are free to find new sources of vital energy. Your creative nature emerges organically when the environment is supportive. You become free to create a new life rulebook that resonates deeply with what you truly believe, and the drive to discover a sense of meaning and purpose in life pushes from inside you. Your life today becomes a playground where you discover what excites you and meaningful ways you can contribute.

Inner Power Practice #12

Be on the look-out for what instinctively grabs your attention, causing you to want to engage. What gets your heart beating a little faster? What do you want to do, but don't allow time and space for? Notice when you are bored: give yourself permission to explore something new and discover what ignites your creative energy. The early stages of finding your true passion are about exploration and following your instinct.

The desire to discover meaning and purpose resides in each of us as part of our life journey and the inner push to grow and transform; it's part of our collective human nature. You alone determine what feels meaningful to you. A life filled with meaning makes the world a more joyous and harmonious place, which is why it's so important to follow that longing. It holds the key to your special and unique contribution to the world. Finding this meaning, a sense of fulfilling a purpose, brings lasting joy and peace.

Sharing your natural gifts and using your innate strengths fills you, too. Releasing your past and living fully in the present, aware of your power to choose a life you deeply desire, is both exhilarating and frightening. Living this way becomes less frightening and more exhilarating as you practice doing it!

The past becomes your hero's story and you are the hero

The great benefit of releasing your past is to know yourself as the hero or heroine of your life. Once you no longer feel like a victim, you are able to move powerfully in the direction you wish. Again, this is a process of removing layers of conditioning teaching you to be the victim or turn your power over to others. Know that if you came from a dysfunctional family, where you were taught to be a victim directly or indirectly, you *can* change this pattern.

Once you shed the victim role and release your attachment to your past, you begin to feel heroic. Overcoming dysfunctional patterns that have been handed down through generations *is* an heroic act! Living in *your* truth feels so powerful and clean; you're free of the debris you may have been carrying around for years, not knowing that you could leave it in the past. You now know that life is what you make it, that you can create anything if you truly desire it from the depths of your heart and soul.

Starting slowly gives you confidence and creates a foundation for you to grow stronger every day. Notice your old habits and patterns; make a list of them, and become determined to change those patterns. Discover your inner truth by spending time alone in reflection, in play, and in soothing, comforting environments. Acknowledge each small change you make, embrace it as your new life, and celebrate every success no matter how small. Celebrate the way you want to live, love how authentically you do it, and your dedication to the entire experience. The more you celebrate and acknowledge your changes, the sooner you will feel you are creating the quality of life you desire.

Journal Inventory #12

Make a list of old habits and patterns you want to change. Watch the tapping video through this portal, https://www.youtube.com/watch?v=aA1bc2q_h3A. Change the energy of old patterns by practicing tapping when you feel emotionally reactive.

You *are* the hero or heroine of your story; the question is – are you ready to make your story a triumphant one?

The past often resides inside you as old losses and disappointments that have not been given good voice or loving attention. As you release your past you will need time and space for feeling, healing and transforming your grief: be sure you have good support to process these losses and disappointments. Learn to grieve well and transform that grief into your own pearls of wisdom. This is our next practice on the Inner Power Wheel.

Guided relaxation exercise for releasing the past

Sit in a comfortable position. Focus your attention on your breath and breathe deeply for a minute. Scan your body for tension and take time to breathe into any tight areas, relaxing them and rejuvenating them with your breath. Spend as much time as you can with this in order to sense a true relaxation within.

Call to mind an issue from your past that troubles you to this day. Notice how your feelings change as you focus on this issue. Bring your attention to your feelings and name them. Notice any thoughts, particularly repetitive thoughts and statements. Use your breath to refocus your attention between feelings and thoughts, and the story the issue creates in your mind. Work on holding feelings and thoughts and the issue collectively in your attention as best you can, moving your attention among these three aspects of your inner experience. Stay with this process for a few minutes. Bring your attention back to your breath. Imagine yourself breathing the energy of this inner story out with your breathing. Stay with the process as long as feels right for you. After a few deep breaths, open your eyes.

Make notes in your journal about the story of the issue in your mind, your thoughts and your feelings. Identify what troubles you most about it right now. Is it the fact it happened? Is it your response to it? Is it someone else's behavior? Are you looking for an apology or do you need to offer one? Are you expecting change in someone else? Are you seeking forgiveness or wanting to offer forgiveness? Is it realistic to be waiting for an apology to let go of the issue and your feelings?

Close your eyes and practice relaxed breathing for a few minutes. Bring your attention to your heart. Ask yourself what you need to resolve this issue inside yourself. Be still and attune to your heart. Ask yourself what action you need to take to bring this issue to closure. Imagine yourself taking that action. Refocus on your breath and open your eyes. Make notes in your journal about your exercise.

Repeat this exercise for all issues from your past that cause you inner unrest today. Do not rush this process. Allow adequate time between sessions for the internal adjustments to take place. More than one session may be needed for certain past issues.

This is essential to becoming free to move on, unencumbered by your past. Since revisiting past traumas and dramas creates deeper vulnerability that may require special attention and assistance, consider consulting a professional counselor or coach at this time.

The Inner Power Wheel

Listen

Accept

Choose

Release

Transform

Create

Live

Return

LIVE YOUR
Inner Power
How to Own
Your Inner Truth,
Activate Your Inner Power
& Make a Positive Impact

Transforming losses
into pearls of wisdom
turns lead into gold, the
alchemist's path. Shedding
accumulated grief frees
you to tap into your essential
wisdom and open to joy.

FIVE

Feel and Transform Grief

Practice 5: Transform

Your ability to feel the fullness of human pain and joy is one of your greatest human assets. In learning to understand, and more importantly to withstand, the intensity of deep grief, the heart becomes the bearer of great wisdom, guiding you into the quality of life that brings peace and joy into the world.

My story

My well of sadness ran so deep. Because I am emotionally and energetically sensitive, I easily connect with what others are feeling. Unconsciously, I took on loved ones' feelings in the past. If I am not careful to honor the difference between other and self, I can repeat this pattern. As I worked with releasing my past, much grieving was involved. My grief muscle was worked on a regular basis: I grieved my parent's troubled marriage; I grieved the stress of my parents' finances; I grieved for the little Laurel who was troubled when adults were not aware of the effect their presence had on the children in the room. I grieved for the sense of loss of a carefree childhood as I became distressed by the disharmony I felt in our home growing up; I grieved the unconscious decision I made in marrying, choosing to push important conflicting feelings into the background. I grieved my inability to speak up for myself and advocate for what I needed; I grieved for the sadness of the world around me as I felt the heaviness of people living in stress, anger, bitterness, frustration – in anything but peace. I grieved for my children when I realized that I had to separate our family. The list feels endless as I write this.

I had been in therapy for a few years and was now going occasionally, when I wanted a 'tune-up.' My life in my new home had stability and joy, and our family life functioned despite the separation. I had been meditating daily for many years, had become a teacher of Tai Chi, and was working on my graduate degree in counseling psychology. At times I felt a little lonely for a loving partnership, but was aware that my time and energy were being used fully in mothering, school, work and in learning about myself – my needs and wants. I was content in a way I had not known before. My healing journey seemed wonderful; I loved my life in nearly every way I could consider.

Despite my satisfying life, the sadness that I'd once chronically felt surfaced with inexplicable intensity, taking me over at times, like a strong ocean undertow. One winter it became a daily practice to sit on my meditation cushion and weep. It was as if I was crying a river that ran in front of me and through my bedroom. If I wasn't careful, I thought, I would float away on that river.

The days turned to weeks and the tears were still flowing. There were days when I wondered if I could continue to hold space for this deep grief, if I could continue to rally better spirits and get through the rest of my day with a semblance of focus and calm. I learned to live deeply in the moment at this time, because I became leery of projecting forward for fear I would lose heart for the experience unfolding. I did not feel depressed as I had before: there was no sense of helplessness or power-lessness, more of a releasing that had no end. I was purging a deep well of sadness that pervaded my being.

I talked to my therapist a few times. I remember vividly talking to a friend when I showed up for a walk with red bleary eyes and her concern was acute. As we walked and talked I shared my 'meditation cushion river of sadness.' I assured her I felt supported. Something in me knew I simply had to remain with my experience, ride it out and let it finish. As the weeks grew to months, I began to wonder if indeed it would ever pass. As I rounded the three-month mark, as suddenly as it seemed to have descended, it lifted.

I re-emerged into life with a new lightness. The feeling of buoyancy was new and a bit intoxicating at times, but I felt solidly grounded in myself. My inner world had a clarity I had not experienced, and the background sadness that had seemed to be my life-long friend was no longer there.

Grieving well was now one of my strengths. As my sadness passed and I had weathered my dark night of the soul passage, I was transformed into a deeper, wiser and profoundly more compassionate version of the woman I was coming to know. My deep grieving opened me to learning how much painful sadness we humans bear – and can bear – while continuing to function and live in an open-hearted manner. Instead of moving away from sadness, it became clearer when it was another's and when it was mine. I could gently remain in the company of another as they grieved, holding space for them to allow their waves to move through and pass. The old steady-state sadness had dissipated to leave me with a clean slate to experience new grief and to encounter another in their grief and sadness. Because I could bear that deep grieving, I came to know that others could too. I wasn't special in my sadness: I simply was willing to feel it, to surrender to the wave that kept washing through me. I knew the wisdom of staying with the experience, leaning into the process and finding a way to hold strong.

The specific losses I encountered have become the pearls of wisdom of living this life, and owning the truth of it. For instance, divorce is painful, but it is also a liberator. It is a teacher of endings and beginnings, of learning to ride the cycle of life, of death. Moving on from divorce becomes wisdom, rebirthing self in new ways. These transformations came through opening fully to grief, feeling it all and searching inside for what I learned by having lived through it. *What do I now know about myself, about life, about others?* I stand tall in the scars of grief as I live the beauty of rebirth beyond loss.

Grieve the old stories of anger and pain

Old hurts control aspects of your life until you consciously heal them. These old hurts show up in a variety of ways: as limiting beliefs about the possibility of a wonderful and fulfilling life; as bitterness when you think how your past life has angered or disappointed you. They are the reactive responses that cause you to protect yourself by not fully experiencing a situation. They are the many ways you have found to say 'no' to life, rather than 'what if?' or 'yes.' When you look at your own hurts and the ways they limit your life, feel them and heal them, your courage expands exponentially.

The quickest route to finding your old stories and beginning the healing process entails noticing when you think and talk about the past. When the past becomes a topic, learn to take inventory of how you are thinking, what you are thinking, and how you feel. Be particularly alert to talking or thinking about past experiences that were painful or made you angry. These old stories determine your future until you no longer feel emotionally embroiled in them.

In my work with individuals, the need for grieving surfaces consistently. We address that need as a client becomes conscious of how their behavior feels 'out of control' and reactive to circumstances. These circumstances illuminate the need for healing, grieving, and discovering how you lost connection with your inner power. We begin the dance of mending buried hurts from the past, and discover how the hurt created a sense of victimhood.

When you start talking about an old hurt, it is often easy to assume a victim role: this was done to me and I am just living with 'it' – whatever 'it' looks like now, perhaps anger, resentment, fear, or blame. Cruel things have been done and you carry the scars of another's anger, neglect or fear. Real healing occurs when you take ownership of the present, a place where you have ultimate control over the condition of your life and your relationships. It is where you empower yourself by saying 'I am not stuck here,' 'I can choose different behavior,' 'I have these feelings and I don't know if they are more about the past or the present' or 'I can change this by changing my old reactions.' Sometimes you decide to walk away from the present and the past, and to do life in a new way.

Journal Inventory #13: Victim Inventory

Where and when do you give up your power?

Where in your life do you feel incapable of change?

When do you stay quiet although you want to speak up?

How do you silence your truth?

How often do you hold back from asking for what you want?

What area(s) of your life do you believe are based on what happened in your past?

Pose these questions and keep coming back to them until you have fully responded.

The following is a concise way to heal from past hurts and become free to live peacefully in the present:

1. Be on the look-out for reactive behaviors – any place where you are stuck in thoughts like 'you are doing this to me,' or 'I can't do anything to change this.' If you see yourself adopting a victim stance, most likely this is about, or tied into, the past.

2. Make space in your life to look at the pattern honestly, searching for old scenarios where you were hurt and may still be carrying the burden of that hurt.

3. Look at the old scenario with fresh eyes, seeing the other person as coming from an unconsciously hurt place as they delivered pain your way.

4. Come back to the present and own your power to make things right for yourself, as in naming the hurt, and forgiving those involved. Self-forgiveness is often a large hurdle: be sure to forgive yourself for carrying the old hurt around for so long, and for allowing it to create ongoing misery. You don't know what you don't know.

5. Practice staying in the present and address what is happening now from a position of strength and compassion, changing current circumstances through your positive presence, rather than habitual reactions.

This process takes time to work through thoroughly, depending on the condition of the old hurt and your willingness, as well as your attention to it. Sometimes it entails cycling through stages of forgiveness until you really put an old hurt to rest. At times, you will find you can release an old grudge or hurt quite quickly, feeling ready, willing and able to let go and move on. You need not feel stuck in a place you don't want to be: you can choose to move into new life with a sense of relief. But not moving fully through the grieving process will leave you stuck somewhere in the past.

Journal Inventory #14

Make a timeline from the earliest age you can recall. Move your memory slowly along your time-line, year by year, recalling all the losses, hurts, grievances, and disappointments you can. Take time to consider what inner work needs to be done to complete your grief process with each one. This process must not be rushed.

You have the power to effect change, always, regardless of whether you want to use that power or not. It takes courage to summon the strength and resilience to own, honestly, every aspect of the life you are living right now. By your willingness and boldness to own your life, you can begin to create the life you want, no longer feeling trapped by your past or an inability to respond more positively to life.

Practice grief

Inevitably, as you accept life on life's terms, you experience loss. The many losses in life provide many opportunities to become proficient at accepting loss when you consciously work through the experiences. You eventually become adept at identifying the cycle of loss, bolder at holding up to intense feelings, and your heart grows stronger with every loss.

In the western culture, we have become proficient at dodging losses by sidestepping into anger or some other emotion; when you feel angry, you feel less vulnerable. In fact, the bravest thing to do is just sit tight and feel the fullness of loss. Feeling anger can be part of the loss cycle, but it is only a part of the full grieving process. Loss is heart-breaking if the thing that is lost means anything to you; to be honest and true to loss – to life – you must let your heart break.

How does it feel when you allow your heart to break? You cry, most likely; at least, tears arrive. You feel a pain in your chest, maybe your throat or stomach, or maybe in your head, but there will be pain, the emotional kind that feels physical when it's intense. It's hard to make the pain go away readily. Time does heal, but only if you consciously decide to flow with the experience and not get stuck along the way.

Time may not banish the pain forever, but it does lessen its intensity. Slowly, you begin to accept a new life without the 'thing' that was lost.

Practicing acceptance is a natural part of the loss/grief cycle. Acceptance means saying 'yes, this is gone,' or 'yes, this is different.' You suffer much more when you try *not* to experience the loss. There are many ways to avoid and resist accepting loss and the pain of grieving. Here is a sample list, some of which you may recognize.

1. For a time you might be frustrated; you might resist pain by ignoring the loss and carrying on regardless. When you stay stuck in ignorance, you often end up more frustrated, maybe indignant, or afraid and unable to think of the loss. You then become the victim of the loss.

2. There is the 'but look what is good about it' tactic to lessen the blow. You take an intellectual approach to the loss process and never really experience the pain in a heartfelt way. This means you get stuck living in your head, out of touch with the intelligence of your full being, burdened with emotional energy that is latent with the loss.

3. You might do the 'justifying' thing, explaining how it's better this way, or focusing on the truth that loss is simply a part of life, using your mind to sidestep the emotional blow of loss. Again, you become the victim of your feelings, unable to navigate your way through the fullness of heartbreak.

Maybe these avoidances help for a time when you feel unable to bear the enormity of some losses. But unless you consciously decide to come back into the feelings of grief, you will be stuck in a place in your mind, or in some kind of anger, walled off from the grief work, and the full cycle of emotional energy that waits in your heart and body. Some part of you numbs to manage the pain, and then becomes unavailable to experience the full joy and richness of life

Journal Inventory #15

Be on the look-out for the methods, habits and patterns you employ to distract yourself from difficult feelings. Make a list. See if you can interrupt the pattern by sitting still, at least briefly, and identifying the feeling you are avoiding. Once identified, see if you can let the feeling arise within you for a time, building your tolerance to it.

This exercise allows you to own your emotional wisdom, and become strong in handling the energy you embody. Eventually, you can begin to talk about the feelings as a way to move them and release their energy.

When you choose not to feel loss for a time, you may compound and confuse the loss, making it more difficult to see, return to, and to feel in its pure form. With my clients, we might spend hours untangling the web that was inadvertently created to avoid feeling loss, to avoid grieving. They usually find themselves stuck in frustration that may have escalated to anger, usually towards someone else, because there is nowhere to keep going with the tangling web of avoiding, disappointment, sadness and grief. Sometimes, they may have become numb from feeling loss and feel frozen, with no feelings able to emerge. Slowly, together, we unweave the web and find the ultimate source. And there it is – a loss.

In general, collectively we lack the fine skills of grieving well. You must learn how to cry more readily, to wail, to grieve, and then rest. You must remember that loss is a natural part of life, as a way of opening your heart to the deepest parts of you.

Grieve the loss consciously and find the gem within

As you learn how to grieve well, you trust life in a new way. First you must experience the full cycle of loss – knowing that new life eventually emerges. After the crying, wailing, grieving passes, you consider the loss from a different perspective. Now you ask – *what of importance have I learned by living through this loss? How can I grow from this wisdom – how have I already grown? How can this wisdom serve me? Serve others? What are the intangible riches of wisdom that I carry from my losses?* These are your life gems.

There are benefits to opening to grief; here are some:

- When you feel the pain fully, and accept the loss, you move into a new life.
- When you feel the pain fully, you no longer set yourself up for getting stuck in a tangled mess of other emotions.
- When you feel the pain fully, you grow your emotional heart muscle, so that you indeed know you can live through deep heartache and into new life. You no longer feel a victim of your emotions.
- When you become comfortable with your own tears, you are able to comfort others as they bear the burdens of loss. You become a healing agent for others.
- When you become more proficient in saying what comforts you, and learn how to comfort, even in silence, your compassion serves others.
- As you learn to handle loss gracefully, you become more graceful in living fully.
- You feel stronger inside because you have sunk into the depths of being human and resurfaced, doing a most difficult thing: facing life anew with the loss still in your heart.

Grieving fully leads you into your authentic power as you live openly through all the cycles of life. You discover inner resources that nothing and no one can take away. You become wise in the truth of the impermanence of human life – the greatest treasure of loss and grief. With this inner discovery, you no longer resist losses, but let go freely. You become an agent of self-transformation from who you were before the loss, to a wiser, stronger, more open-hearted 'you' after the loss. This is what it means to feel and transform grief, becoming strong medicine for the world around you.

Journal Inventory #16

Go back to your Journal Inventory #14. Identify the wisdom gained from each loss you recorded. Create a new page, journal or book, or perhaps a collage or other artwork, to commemorate your wisdom gained through living fully.

Hold space for others in grief

Holding space for another person is an unselfish act of giving; it is an act of presence. What does holding space mean? It means you bring your full attention and being into the moment when you are with someone. It means setting aside your mental process for a time, and disengaging from your emotional process. This does not mean that you don't feel anything: you simply let the emotion or feeling arise, but continue to give good attention to the other, so that their experience is allowed in its fullness. You usually do not speak, but rather make good eye contact (unless intuitively you feel it is best not to). Your body language reflects that you are open and available. Speak briefly if a question is asked directly, keeping your attention on the other person until the time is complete. Any speaking is usually reassurance; just a reminder that you are right here and listening. Holding space is complete when the other person arrives at a place that feels 'finished' to them, when there is a sense of completion to the process they are sharing. You will likely 'feel' this completion too; usually a sense of emptiness and gratefulness arises. A feeling of peace also emerges as they let go of what burdened them.

Doesn't that sound good? Who doesn't want that kind of loving attention? Do you? Unfortunately, you may have been conditioned to resist or feel discomfort with this loving attention. You may not be accustomed to having such undivided attention and time offered freely from another. You can recondition yourself to enjoy this experience, as you find it, learning to let go in the safe space held by another; similarly, you can learn and practice the skill of holding space for another.

What does it take to gain this skill? Willingness: you must be willing to let go of your own needs and wants for a time to offer space to another completely. This might mean a shift in how you normally operate in the world; learning to let go of self-interests and of being right; letting go of wanting equal time, and getting your opinions into the experience. It means cultivating the practice of simply being with another; the only agenda is being present and attending to their needs through undivided attention. You develop a tolerance for letting another feel their feelings without the need to fix, change or control. This requires learning to hold your heart open while you allow and acknowledge. Becoming proficient in this takes practice.

When you give the gift of holding space freely, you also receive. You, like many of us, may have been conditioned to believe that taking care of others means tedious work. If so, you may often do *more* than is truly helpful. You will experience a sense of wonder that, not only are you capable of this loving kindness, but it really is this 'simple' to be supportive and caring. Holding space also requires that you have paid loving attention to what needs healing and soothing within you, so that you can let go and offer your attention fully to the other person. I think this is the key to unlocking your innate ability to hold space for another – finding the loving space you deeply want from those who willingly give it.

Inner Power Practice #13

Begin your practice of holding space for another as soon as possible. Challenge yourself to do it today if possible. Practicing in small ways gets you ready for a more intense experience when someone is more emotional. For now, be an active listener without judging, adding an opinion or commenting after someone speaks. You might say 'I really hear you,' or 'I get what you are saying,' something that affirms you heard without adding anything to what they said. This might feel uncomfortable at first. In time the benefits will emerge as you relax into the experience.

The wise you that emerges from the ability to grieve

When you shy away from fully experiencing grief and pain, you lose an opportunity to become strong and healthy emotionally. Opening fully to the grieving process means you will experience emotional pain, pain that sometimes seems unbearable. Through these experiences, you grow emotionally; you must not stunt your loss experiences by turning away from them. Learning to lean into, and through them is an invaluable life skill that transforms your grief into inner wisdom and strength.

Developing the strength to stay with loss and resultant feelings empowers you with inner wisdom. This wisdom comes from searching the loss for the beauty of what was gained from the experience. Sometimes you don't recognize a gift in your life until it is gone: wisdom may be hard to discover amidst the pain during the early grieving stages, but you uncover the real gifts in time. Truncating the loss experience without finding the hidden gem is a missed opportunity to understand your life in its totality.

When you honor every aspect of your life, you also honor the losses. Emotional pain hurts. Extreme emotional pain can feel intolerable.

Learning to discern tolerable pain from intolerable pain may require assistance. When you have not been allowed and encouraged to feel your deep sadness it lies within, perhaps expressing itself as depression.

As you identify with the depressed mood, the inner grief may no longer be connected to a tangible loss. The original feeling morphs into an all-pervasive sense of heaviness. In listening to your deeper inner feelings, you may reconnect individually with each life loss, grieving every one properly; engaging in life anew without the heaviness of the losses then becomes possible.

Our western culture minimizes loss, which means many of us do not know what healthy grieving looks like. There is no formula for how long it takes to grieve a loss or any 'right' way to grieve fully. Riding the waves of your grief requires staying with all your feelings, allowing the ebb and flow of sadness – at times anger – until eventually a sense of new life beyond the loss emerges. You will need to call on your inherent inner strength; support, kindness and love are also essential to a healthy grieving process. Relying on others' strength to carry you through when you feel weak creates interdependence, which feels positive as you experience mutual giving and receiving. You learn to be dependent and strong, and others can then depend on you for this kind of support.

With your growing heart and ability to navigate your full emotional experience more readily, it is essential to create healthy, flexible boundaries. Creating boundaries means you structure life carefully and consciously, which elevates your good-enough life to one of passion, excitement, joy, peace, adventure – anything you want it to be. Let's explore the art of setting healthy, flexible boundaries.

Guided relaxation exercise for healing and transforming grief

Sit in a comfortable position. Focus on your breathing, taking relaxed and deep breaths as you attend to this process. Utilize your breath to focus on any tension in your body, relaxing and releasing the tension through directed breathing.

Bring to mind something that makes you sad. Take time to focus on your feelings and the issue; allow any tears that arise to be expressed. Stay with this for a few minutes. Bring your attention back to your breath and calm yourself through relaxed and attentive breathing. Now ask yourself what you had, and no longer have, that elicited this particular sadness. Or what do you want to experience, that you do not, that is connected to this sadness? Be as specific as you can in the identifying process. Take a few deep breaths and open your eyes. Make notes.

Close your eyes and reconnect with your relaxed breathing. Focus on your heart. Ask yourself what you had before the loss. What have you learned about yourself by being with your sadness fully? Ask yourself what this sadness tells you about what you want in life. Feel gratitude for anything you have gained from this grief. Be sure to acknowledge inwardly the experience of *having* before the loss occurred. Be sure to acknowledge fully the deeper understanding you have of yourself through feeling this grief. Take three deep breaths and open your eyes. Make notes.

Take time to move through your history, going thoroughly through the disappointments, hurts, angers, and betrayals. Give space and time to grieve each one properly so that you may discover your learning, your pearls of wisdom. Find support for the deep grieving, someone who can hold space fully and give healthy support. Consciously choose to transform your grief into wisdom.

If you experienced trauma or significant loss in your past, it is vital you do a more in-depth study and gain a greater understanding of grieving. This is a time to consider working with a professional, someone who has experience guiding and supporting the grief process. I recommend reading the book, "On Grief and Grieving" by Elisabeth Kubler-Ross and David Kessler. This book offers a thorough explanation of the grieving cycle and explores the world of grief in inspirational detail.

The Inner Power Wheel

Listen

Accept

Choose

Release

Transform

Create

Live

Return

LIVE YOUR
Inner Power
How to Own
Your Inner Truth,
Activate Your Inner Power
& Make a Positive Impact

With consciousness
of bringing life into form
through you, you choose
carefully your inner and
outer boundaries. This
practice harnesses energy
and power in service to
your desires.

SIX

Create Flexible, Healthy Boundaries

Practice 6: Create

When you contain your life in proper order, your boundaries reflect who you are and what you are creating. This containment holds you safe and secure, allowing you to grow fluidly, trusting your expanding attunement to life.

My story

As I choose consciously, with knowledge of my deeper desires, I know it is my responsibility alone to create my experiences, and yet I do this in and with the world around me. I co-create with life every day now. As I grow stronger and choose to engage with others in a heartfelt way, I find my connections growing in the world, bringing more opportunities, more invitations and more interests. Suddenly, I am overextending myself with agreeing to more than my calendar and energy can comfortably manage. My old habit of people-pleasing has made a re-entry but with a new twist. There is much that pleases me and I want to experience it all!

The art of boundary setting takes major awareness and effort as my life blossoms into a garden of good activities. I cannot say yes to everyone and everything without exhausting myself, and feeling resentful of participating beyond what is healthy for me. I want to honor the limits of my energy, the need for enough 'alone time,' and the intimacy I desire in my treasured relationships. To balance these aspects of my life well, being conscious and careful in what I agree to is a must! In order to break the habit of 'yessing,' I begin by saying 'I need to think about that; let me get back to you. Thanks for asking and including me.' Then I consider everything I've already committed to and decide whether this event or engagement fits well into my life.

As I come to know myself well, I realize I hold myself to high standards. I want to give my best in all my relationships, showing compassion and kindness. This means I need to be mindful of whether I can indeed follow through in a way I will feel good about. I have learned to say up front how busy I am, and express my limits in the project from the beginning. I consider everything I say 'yes' to in light of what is within my ability to execute. I don't want to set myself up to feel guilty, exhausted, burned out, or embarrassed because I am not giving what feels honorable and true to me.

The next step was to learn how to say 'no' on the spot. Saying 'no' well is an art in itself. It feels good to be wanted, to have my presence desired, so I want to say 'yes' in appreciation. I can experience these feelings and still say no. After much practice, I have made peace with saying no to others when I already have a full schedule. I thank people right away for their invitation, and tell them I am saying no because my time is chock-full. I wish them a wonderful experience as well!

My life to me is like a canvas I am always painting. The forms of my life are my work, my relationships, my home, my recreation and my alone time. For my life to flow pleasantly I must determine boundaries for each aspect of my life and set the limits that I need to keep it all moving well and joyfully. My deepest responsibility is to honor the path

I am walking consciously now, keeping my energy high, my attitude positive and maintaining my motivation to experience life to its fullest. Only I can create these inner conditions for a joyful life experience and I do it through creating healthy, flexible boundaries. Then I communicate them to the best of my ability.

What are boundaries?

Boundaries are the borders or structures you implement in your life, physically and metaphorically. They are the edges that create the 'form' of your life. The intent of healthy boundaries is to keep you safe while allowing for growth, recognizing that fluidity, change, and restructuring are all important parts of living a conscious life. Choosing healthy, flexible boundaries permits optimal health and self-expression. Your life will take on new form many times when you live with conscious intention, so your boundaries must be flexible.

Living in a conscious and intentional manner inherently produces health by embodying the desire for ongoing growth. When you are connected to your inner life force, which desires regeneration and expansion, you generally make healthy choices that induce vibrancy and excitement. Unfortunately, you aren't necessarily conditioned to make these kinds of choices; you may be conditioned to make 'safe,' 'financially prudent,' and 'socially acceptable' choices. Or your conditioning may have caused you to make 'desperate,' 'unwise,' or 'irrational' choices from learning unhealthy boundaries in the environments you first experienced. This kind of conditioning can move you *away* from what your inner life force wants to move you *towards*. To 'live your inner power' means to reconnect with the inner life force that guides you to make healthy choices in alignment with your highest Self. You are the change agent that brings your highest form of life into being.

When you bring your highest Self into form, you live your passion and your purpose and become a creative, healing force in the world. That quality of energy exists within you, within me, within all of us. We cannot act on that life force when we are disconnected from it. As you mature, the goal is to become ever more congruent with this life force that will lead you into, as Oprah Winfrey would say, 'your best life.'

What would your best life look like? Just for today? You need not know about ten years from now, unless you feel ready to consciously create that far forward. Beginning today is of the essence. As you consciously claim the choices your heart and soul really want, your life will naturally organize towards these inner truths and desires. New desires emerge as you change and grow that mean reorganizing your boundaries. Begin where you are now and the rest will follow and flow with time and practice.

Simply make small choices that create the boundaries of your life – as you want it today. This form expresses the authentic you, allows you to relax into the truth of being you, and causes you to be excited about getting up each day! This may mean some tough choices, choices that create change both for you and those with whom you are in relationship.

The goal is to make these choices from a heart-centered and clear place so that you feel good about them and the direction you are heading. The choices create boundaries, and the boundaries create experience. When you accept more responsibility for every aspect of your life, you co-create with life around you in new and exciting ways.

Early boundary setting

When you were very young, crying and screaming was how you got what you needed to survive. You cried out when you were hungry. You cried out when you wanted to feel dry and clean. You cried out when you didn't feel good and needed help. You cried out when you needed attention and love. Eventually you learned to speak; *asking* became the way to communicate needs and desires. The responses you got – how, when and with what kind of emotional energy – created the patterns of boundary setting as you grew.

If you didn't consistently get what you needed, your method of getting attention and creating boundaries may be a mess of unhealthy and indirect approaches. These continue until you discover more mature and effective ways to interact. Whenever I see adults making a scene of any kind in public, I think: 'This person didn't learn to get their needs met in a healthy way.' They never learned how to communicate their needs well and work through the process to resolution. They are still behaving from 'the child within,' attempting to get attention. Usually, the result is unpleasant for all involved.

An immature manner of boundary setting is rigid boundary-setting: the black-and-white version, or the all-or-nothing method. This pattern arises in response to having lived in an unsafe environment, emotionally, mentally or physically. You now need strong walls for safety; they may be unconscious, often immobile, keeping out the 'bad' but also limiting the good.

Journal Inventory #17

Write in an unedited manner for a while, focusing on what you learned about boundaries growing up. See if you can identify any patterns of how you get what you want and need now that seem immature or unhealthy. Think about recent situations in which you wanted something and write about how you went about making that happen.

This exercise is meant to increase your consciousness around your current habits and patterns. Withholding judgment and simply noticing is important in this process, to encourage less conscious patterns to come into your field of awareness.

Sadly, your boundaries may not support a deep connection with Self, the part of you that knows what feels meaningful and fulfilling. In order to create this kind of life, give yourself permission to have time alone, time to commune quietly with yourself to discover what you like, what you want, and who you really are on the inside. You may have been conditioned to believe it your role to be available to others all the time. Perhaps you have been conditioned to organize life around others' schedules. Creating boundaries that give Self the time to be heard and known can mean letting go of some responsibilities, some old patterns, even some relationships if they drain you without nurturing those important aspects of yourself that you now want to develop. Such shifts require courage, time and a new commitment to Self.

As you develop a sense of internal safety and a deep connection to your inner power (the power that allows you to say yes and no in alignment with your truth), new boundaries can be created. This is an important aspect of creating the life you deeply desire. Boundaries, when they stay firmly intact without reconsideration over time, can limit your potential to experience life and achieve what you want. Boundaries not only keep out the life you don't want, but can inadvertently set limits to acknowledging and attaining what you do want. The goal is to feel that you have the power to determine your boundaries and change them at will.

You may not feel you have the power to change boundaries in specific areas or relationships. You may perceive that life determines your boundaries rather than you choosing them. This pattern comes from your early life experiences, and what your life thus far has taught you. Normally, we learn boundary-setting skills in the home in which we are raised and through significant early relationships. It can be helpful to reflect on the lessons you learned directly and indirectly during your formative years. Unhealthy experiences and role modeling in your past makes healthy boundary setting a hard task, but not an impossible one. Practice creates proficiency.

The mature path of compassion and boundaries

The mature path of getting needs met is to involve your heart and clear mind through intentional conscious choice. This includes communicating well and directly. Living the life you deeply desire happens purposefully by making each choice *in line* with what you deeply desire. A mature approach to setting boundaries means asking for what you want and need, saying no and yes in alignment with your inner truth and desires. Anger is rarely a theme because you have established a life that supports what you want and you have the tools to build a fulfilling life. When anger does arise, ask yourself if the situation requires altering your boundaries. If you don't know how to set boundaries in a comfortable and confident manner yet, you can learn. I like to think of boundary setting as an art form: you are creating the image, the masterpiece that is your life. This image changes as you grow and express different aspects of yourself in new ways. It's courageous to continually claim what will fulfill you.

Reviewing boundaries becomes a best practice exercise, a way of life when you live consciously and intentionally. Start by looking at your life as it is right now. Here is a template to use for considering the boundaries you have now, how you got here and where you want to go next. Identify an area of your life:

1. Describe the condition of this area of your life right now.
2. What made you begin this experience and how has it changed?
3. How have you grown or changed since this started?
4. What have you learned from this experience?
5. If you could wave a magic wand and change this, what would it look like now?
6. What small step can you take right now to bring you in closer alignment with this change?
7. Make a plan of change: create steps to move into and through the change you want in this experience.
8. Execute the plan, modifying it as needed, depending on what happens.

Examining the boundaries you have put (or not put) in place is a crucial aspect of acknowledging the life you have created. It is important to spend time considering your personal boundaries, relationship boundaries, work life boundaries, your creative boundaries and your inner boundaries. Making conscious boundary choices can alter your life flow in ways that ultimately support your best interests, as well as those of the world around you. It means creating a life in alignment with your inner truth and your inner passions. In my experience, everyone wins in this situation. When you bring a weak, watered-down version of yourself to any experience, no one benefits; when you bring a passionate, creative, energetic self into your life experience, everyone benefits.

Creating boundaries means deciding what you want, communicating what you want to others and then acting on it – aligning thought, word and deed. There is no 'right' way to do this. I have learned that doing it, and doing it well are both essential to living well and feeling fulfilled. When I set boundaries poorly, by being unclear or aggressive in communicating them, I feel guilty or frustrated. I continue to learn through my own personal growth how important it is to practice and become proficient at setting boundaries clearly and compassionately.

Peace comes through the creation of a life of your own choosing, as well as accepting life as it is in this moment. This is the paradox of boundary setting: *we control what we can, and enter a flow beyond our individual control.* This is where the great mystery lies – attuning to the universal flow of abundance and joy by artfully placing your boundaries precisely where you want them.

Inner Power Practice #14: Fine-tuning Your Boundaries

Choose one area of your life you know you want to change or grow. Challenge yourself to change some boundary. Perhaps it's the frequency of engagement; perhaps it's how often you think about it. Perhaps it's halting completely. Make a decision and act on it.

Create positive relationships by intentionally changing boundaries

When you are unhappy with the quality of any relationship, you must decide to be the agent of change by instituting new boundaries. Waiting for anyone else to change their behavior or attitude leaves the quality of your life in someone else's hands. If you are in a relationship where repeated unpleasant patterns occur, acknowledge that by participating, even if only by allowing, you are part of maintaining the existence of those patterns. Any painful, neglectful or cruel actions require response, even if the response is to end the relationship. The following suggestions can lead you to becoming more powerful in handling difficult people, and in working with your internal world as you determine which relationships to cultivate or release.

First, no retaliatory actions will ever make you feel good about yourself, or help build the quality of relationship you are ultimately seeking. Only setting healthy, appropriate boundaries will change the relationship for the better. Anyone who uses their knowledge of you for cruelty, even unconsciously, needs to be put in a place in your life where they cannot damage you. You serve no one in making yourself available to someone for hurtful interactions. Anyone with a conscience feels guilty about cruel behavior; emotionally mature and responsible individuals change hurtful behaviors. If someone doesn't recognize their cruel behavior and you do, acknowledging your differing values is the first step in changing the relationship and moving towards a resolution.

Think of your circle of friends and family as a bull's-eye; move dangerous, disrespectful people outward until they cannot reach you to hurt you. This might mean moving them completely out of your circle.

Second, it is personally beneficial to examine the reasons you have not set boundaries to stop the activity or end the relationship. You can gain wisdom through identifying old patterns and family rules, and considering what patterns and rules you want in your life *today*. Here are some questions to consider as you search for the inner reasons you continue unhealthy relationships or remain in undesirable experiences:

1. Are you a conflict avoider? If you find you cannot handle conflict, it would be helpful to learn skills in this area.

2. Are you afraid of losing the relationship(s) altogether? Do you prefer hurtful relationships to none?

3. Are you afraid of feeling alone or lonely? We feel most alone when we do not know ourselves, when we feel our *real* self is not seen by others. Do you know who you really are, and are you behaving accordingly?

4. Deep inside, do you believe you deserve to be treated poorly or have the experience you are having? Have you developed an inability to value yourself through maintaining these relationships, perhaps acting badly in return, perpetuating the unhealthy experience?

5. Is laziness, resignation, or bitterness preventing you from bothering to attempt change? Are you just accepting the situation and taking on a victim stance? How have you benefited from giving up your power to change the situation?

Answering these questions can give you insight and ultimately the power to make the changes you desire.

Journal Inventory # 18

Identify your boundary setting patterns:

- Avoiding conflict
- Fear of losing relationships

- Frequent feelings of loneliness
- Fear of being alone
- Unworthy of being treated with love and respect
- Resigned to the quality of relationships you have

Write in an unedited way about these patterns.

Watch the video on tapping at this link – https://www. youtube.com/watch?v=aA1bc2q_h3A. Tap and release the charge around your old patterns and start new, positive inner dialogue and habits.

Third, in order to surround yourself with high quality relationships, you must know and live by your true Self. Embody your values and truth rigorously. If you say a certain behavior feels wrong to you, don't behave that way yourself. For instance, if you value kindness, behave kindly and accept no less from others. When you value truth, speak honestly – consistently – and accept no less from others. If you want and value respect, behave respectfully with everyone, and accept no less from others. When you value love, behave lovingly and seek loving people to surround you.

I have found through years of living my values rigorously that the more I behave in line with my values, the more naturally those I am not compatible with disengage from my life, and not necessarily with much drama. A mutual lack of interest develops when I grow and others remain the same, or if they change and I do not. The relationship comes to its organic conclusion, having lived out its usefulness.

Accepting less from others reflects a belief that *they are less*: that you believe they cannot behave more kindly, respectfully, truthfully, lovingly. Accepting less from others reflects that you feel deserving of poor treatment, ultimately assisting the behavior's continuity. You are the cup that holds what another pours forth; if you choose to be the cup, you are part of what keeps the behavior pouring out. You can choose to withdraw from the process, and be true to your values and beliefs by creating a boundary that says, no more – no more with me.

Creating a fulfilling life includes having people in your world who respect and value you. It is difficult to have the energy or interest to cultivate change when you are managing unhealthy relationships; making changes is essential if you are in unhealthy friendships, marriages or family ties. As the creator of your boundaries, you willingly take on the responsibility of building healthy, harmonious and prosperous relationships and experiences.

Forgiving and boundaries

When you experience hurt and anger in relationships it is important to acknowledge all the feelings directly and set healthy boundaries accordingly. Part of becoming mature and expanding the capacity of a loving heart comes through practicing forgiveness. Depending on the intensity of pain or anger you feel, forgiving can be a challenge, but it is the path to engaging life to its fullest, unencumbered by your past, and with an open heart.

If forgiveness is a topic you need to give extra time and attention to, reading the many wonderful books on it can be enlightening. One of my personal favorites is "Forgiveness, A Bold Choice for a Peaceful Heart" by Robin Casarjian. Here are my steps to forgiveness:

1. **Acknowledge your feelings.** Identify and accept them without judgment. Write about them. Talk it over with a professional or unbiased party who will not get involved in the situation, but rather help you accept and own your feelings about what happened.

2. **Acknowledge the situation.** Review the situation as a series of facts that happened. Practice accepting the truth of the situation in its entirety. Do not dramatize or embellish; only the events and actions are important here. This helps you see it more as a 'story' that happened in your life, with less emotional stress.

3. **Notice how the violation occurred.** State clearly to yourself how you feel violated by this person. Search your personal value system to identify which values you hold high that were violated by this experience. Be specific about how this particular experience was wrong for you; if you committed a transgression against another, be clear about how you violated your own values.

4. **Change your boundaries to honor what is important and alleviate further anger.** This is critical for building new trust, both in yourself, and in the other if you decide to continue the relationship. It is difficult to end feelings of anger if you feel vulnerable to more transgressions. The new boundary you set is meant to give you time to recover from the feelings and to get clear on what you desire going forward. You may need a testing period to determine if you want to continue the relationship and if you can build new trust; some violations take us beyond the point where we want to continue.

5. **Forgive the transgression.** How do you soften your heart and allow a letting go to take place? It must be done gently, again and again, as many times as it takes to release the bitterness and any anger. Remember that the interaction, the hurt, and the boundary violation are over: what you are forgiving is in the past, what you are letting be, is done. Hold your part in the experience in your heart and soften to this too. Recall what you were struggling with at the time. See it ALL as complete. Allow it all inside; forgive the lack of consciousness around everyone's choices. Each time anger or bitterness surfaces, open your heart and remember it is all in the past. Accept each individual's part in it, allow it all, and forgive all for not being kinder, more aware, more forthright, whatever else comes up that feels as if it fell short in the situation. And remember it is done. Choose to forgive again, as long as you need to, until the bitterness and anger are finally washed away.

Inner Power Practice #15:
Daily forgiveness meditation

....

Sit quietly and let your attention come to your heart. Review your past day for any feelings of hurt, betrayal or disappointment. Ask yourself what part you played in the experience. Breathe into your heart and seek full awareness of what happened. Ask yourself if new boundaries would serve you now. Hold the situation in your heart and call inwardly for the feelings of forgiveness and letting go to emerge. Just sit with the feeling and the situation. Breathe consciously a few times before you finish. Journal as needed about how to take action in alignment with what your heart and self want now.

Not forgiving means you continue to suffer. You use precious energy in remaining constricted somewhere inside, holding yourself closed off to being finished with what happened. You forgo your opportunity to move into new life free from your past, open to the present and a wonderful future. Forgiveness is the bold and courageous choice. It is the ultimate task of boundary setting.

Having set new boundaries, those that are healthy and allow you to engage optimally in the world, you are now ready to cultivate the practice of living through the heart – using your emotional energy to fuel your deepest desires. You are in constant connection with the deepest aspects of yourself that know what will bring you, and the world around you, the greatest life satisfaction. You discover how you want to serve the world with your unique gifts and talents. Let's delve into living through the heart.

Guided relaxation exercise
for creating healthy, flexible boundaries

Sit or lie in a comfortable position. Focus on your breathing and utilize your breath to relax any tension in your body. Bring your attention to your thoughts, noticing any that arise spontaneously. Imagine your thoughts like a river flowing in front of you. Watch them as they arise and attempt to remain disengaged from them. Instead, look at each thought as moving away as you do not connect to it.

Bring your attention to your emotional state. Notice any emotions that arise with thoughts. Refocus on your breath. Take three deep breaths and open your eyes. Make notes of anything you noticed.

Close your eyes; focus on your breath. Take three deep breaths. Bring to mind the relationship in your life that you find most troubling. Imagine yourself standing next to this person. Imagine looking directly at them in your mind's eye. Now begin to walk away from them, backwards, slowly, until you feel you have moved far enough away that the relationship no longer disturbs you. Bring your attention to your breath and focus on your heart. Ask yourself, what do I want from this relationship? What keeps me engaged with this person? What must I do to make peace with this relationship? Sit quietly with these questions as long as necessary. Refocus on your breathing. Take three deep breaths and open your eyes. Make notes about your exercise.

Take time to practice forgiving in all areas of your life until you can keep a calm and peaceful heart about all past traumas and transgressions. Purposefully take time to process losses. Allow yourself to consciously create boundaries around the time spent healing your past, and free yourself to move forward as you deeply desire. With this commitment of time to experience fully your loss and grief, you become less likely to erupt suddenly at an inopportune time. Dedicate yourself to freely moving forward with an open, healed heart.

The Inner Power Wheel

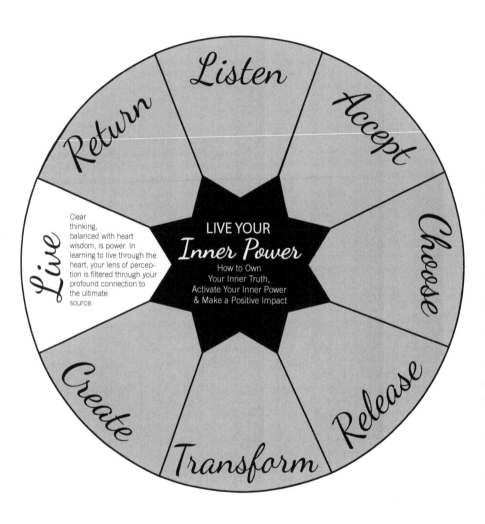

Listen

Accept

Choose

Release

Transform

Create

Live

Return

Clear thinking, balanced with heart wisdom, is power. In learning to live through the heart, your lens of perception is filtered through your profound connection to the ultimate source.

LIVE YOUR
Inner Power
How to Own
Your Inner Truth,
Activate Your Inner Power
& Make a Positive Impact

SEVEN

Live Through the Heart

Practice 7: Live

When you trust and value yourself, you recognize the wisdom of your heart and the necessity of remaining in constant connection with this inner sensitivity, that which leads you into greater truth and knowledge, manifesting greater peace for all of life.

My story

When I reflect on the inner mess that I made in my life through unconscious choices, I see so clearly the misalignment of my heart and my mind. I remember my fears, and the unconsciously driven security I sought when I was younger. What did I know back then about life and about myself? I knew I needed to figure out how to navigate life on my own because it was time to leave the home I had grown up in: the help I needed wasn't going to be found there. My first marriage couldn't help but be affected by these truths. It would have served me well to have found a way to live on my own for a time, but I had no idea how to get there. So I married. There was no conscious intention to use or hurt my ex-husband – I loved him.

My first husband is a kind and thoughtful man. He loves his children and he loved me with a deep devotion. His second wife now enjoys that devotion and thoughtfulness. The depth our connection lacked was something I needed. I needed, and deeply wanted, to feel fulfilled and able to express all of myself in and through my primary relationship. Following my heart brought me into my marriage and it also led me out of it. Living through my heart meant trusting that the messages coming from my heart had value and were worthy of my full attention.

In order to leave my first marriage well I needed to address the imbalances left from growing up when I had felt disempowered to move forward with full consciousness. I needed to address my reactive behaviors and deal with the impact my past had on my inner world and my choices. This was a process of going into my heart, mourning the losses, and also opening to the joy of the life I deeply wanted. Without doing those things, I wasn't fully embracing how the heart experiences life: it holds both our joys and our sorrows.

My heartfelt wisdom came through experiencing, *feeling*, all the losses I had accumulated along my path but had not let myself fully feel, acknowledge and understand. My grieving allowed me to open to aspects of my heart I had walled up because I didn't know how to hold them in my consciousness without being disappointed as I looked around my life and felt I had betrayed myself and others. My healing and the emergent authentic power to act in alignment with my heart came after grieving well and embracing what my heart deeply desired.

My desire for a loving, authentic partnership with a man, who wanted the depth and understanding of self that I was seeking, was a deep want only I could bring about. I had to leave the safe marriage to find the soulful marriage. I needed to feel what my heart wanted and then align my behavior and intentions accordingly. This process took some time, and living through my heart guided me well. Aligning word, thought and deed with my heartfelt wisdom transformed my life into the soulful experience I now enjoy.

Conditioned to live through the mind

We have all been conditioned to live through the mind. From the moment we set foot in school, the emphasis is on using your mind well. All reward systems are set up according to how you excel or exceed in academics, in the intellectual process. By the time I was thirty years old, despite being a highly sensitive, emotional person, my mind – the mental realm – was where my important decisions were made, often ignoring the valuable information held in my full being, especially my heart.

Much of the information my being sent me early in life was tinged with sadness and a sense of helplessness. I imagine that may have been why I attempted to keep disconnected from my heart. Living through the heart can be painful at times, because you risk the vulnerability of your inner self, the truth of knowing all you are feeling. Ultimately, living through the heart offers the opportunity to experience great joy and love; a conscious connection with your heart must be made for this to occur.

Because the cultural conditioning to be mentally empowered is so strong, you may find your inner connection to your heart is weak. If this is true, you must take time to strengthen your conscious heart connection. In some ways, the process is straightforward: you pay attention to your feelings, and literally put your attention into your heart area on a regular basis; you learn the language of emotions and love. You do this purposefully.

Without understanding emotions and feelings, your mind-made world can cause you misery, boredom, or a sense of emptiness. When the mind rules without heart knowledge, you are disengaged from an essential aspect of your being, and the wisdom it carries for happiness and peace, for fulfillment and joy. The wisdom of the heart, serviced well by a purposefully directed mind, is a powerful combination that fuels your life into meaning and fulfillment. The balance of heart and mind is essential to healthy choices and life development.

Finding that balance in our culture can be tricky, since we are encouraged to seek life direction through our mind; however, living too much in your head leads to a sense of confusion. On the other hand, living your life based solely on emotional content can feel reckless. Tempered thinking, fueled by clear, pure emotion, leads to productive, balanced choices. Balancing heart and mind is the project of a lifetime: you do not finish until you draw your last breath. Your mental energy and emotional energy surge within you: a healthy adult finds expression for both these life forces. Heartfelt living entails finding that balance, learning to flow in the fullness of your inner life and the world around you.

Without the heart playing an integral part in your decision-making process, your life feels subtly (or blatantly) empty, devoid of heartfelt meaning. Attune to the wisdom of your heart, learn its language, speak and trust this inner wisdom.

At times your inner wisdom can recommend difficult and painful choices. Understandably, we avoid them – it's not fun making difficult, painful choices! But doing so actually builds the balanced heart-mind connection, while avoidance disconnects you from your heartfelt power. As you live through the heart, you become more honest, leading you to feel more authentically powerful. Perhaps you have feared just the opposite: one cultural myth is that being emotional and heart-centered shows weakness. What a misnomer! The strongest people I know are heart-centered and fully experience their emotional lives.

Inner Power Practice #16

Pay daily attention to your heart. Notice when you are absorbed in your thoughts. The key is noticing when your life suddenly seems like a drama. Practice tuning in to your heart versus playing out mental stories and repeating thoughts through your mind. You will find your power lies in how you experience the current moment not in how you relate to the future or the past. For today, remember to breathe into your heart a few times throughout the day, check in with your feelings, and sense into your presence. Remind yourself that thoughts are less important than the present experience.

Express through the heart

When you try to navigate life without tuning into your emotional world – minus your full inner guidance system – you leave behind your most effective fuel. Your emotions, when understood as an expression of your deeper inner world, can fuel and empower you, keeping you connected to a deep aspect of your inner truth. Cut off from your emotional life, you experience inner unrest and incongruity, as do those around you when they tune into your energy.

When emotions like passion, joy, and excitement run through your inner world, your quality of life generally feels uplifting and positive. When emotions like anger, sadness and guilt run through your being, life generally feels difficult and challenging.

Learning to cultivate particular emotional states empowers you with the fuel of your choice, and it becomes easier and more natural with practice. Clearing inner space for purposeful cultivation may be challenging, depending on your present emotional habits and patterns. Here is the system I use to cultivate my inner landscape and elicit the emotions I want more of:

1. Practice allowing all emotion to arise naturally; simply identify the feelings. Make this a daily practice.

2. Pay attention to your physical body and the signals it gives you via the different emotions you experience, i.e., how you physically experience different feeling states.

3. Connect with the internal and external triggers for your emotions. What thoughts bring about anger, joy, and guilt? What

interactions stimulate disappoint, happiness and peace? Take inventory and understand your personal inclinations.

4. Identify what you like to feel and experience. What emotional states do you want to cultivate? What about those states do you like? What activities elicit more of this emotional energy?

You may have been conditioned to believe you can't control your emotions: in some respects this is true. I am not advocating that you control your emotions, but you can control how you respond. When you are emotionally reactive to an experience, it usually indicates old conditioning that needs release, so that you may experience a more tempered and empowered response to life. The feelings you enjoy increase as you heal old wounds, practice creating new boundaries, and make more conscious choices in a day-to-day way.

Practice living through the heart

When you discover you've been disconnected from the valuable information your heart offers, it can feel like an enormous loss. When I started valuing the tenderness of my heart, tuning in to my intuition, and listening for the guidance pulsing from my heart, I felt I was waking up from a slumber. In that slumber, I had made choices that were not well-suited to the 'me' I was coming to know.

Aware that I had made choices while disregarding important information my heart held, I felt I had betrayed myself and others. The guilt was staggering at times. I directed my efforts back to self-acceptance and to withholding judgment toward myself – 'I didn't know what I didn't know back then.' Staying still with myself, allowing my heartfelt feelings to emerge and be recognized, I made new choices in alignment with my heart's true desires.

Living through the heart is an art that you hone with time and experience. In the early stages, you learn to identify emotions and feelings accurately. What exactly does anger feel like, and its many variations:

frustration, indignation, irritation, and rage? How do they feel in my body, and how do I express them in a healthy way, honoring what my feelings indicate? When you practice living through the heart, you become proficient at identifying emotions and the resultant feelings, you are able to name them, determine what triggered them, and what useful information they offer. This takes time. And all of it is extremely empowering.

Journal Inventory #19

Create a journal with these sections: Fear, Joy, Sadness, and Anger.

List all the variations of these emotional states, describing the many ways they arise in you. Identify what triggers the different emotions and feelings. Describe how the feelings are manifested in your physical body. What are the sensations and sensitivities associated with different emotions?

A sense of empowerment arises, because suddenly you know yourself in a much deeper, more authentic manner. You are able to 'own' what you feel, 'own' what the feelings indicate about your values, your life desires, and your passions. All this wisdom helps you identify choices that will lead to a fulfilling and meaningful life. Without this vital information, it can seem as if you are stabbing about aimlessly, trying to determine what might make you truly 'happy,' what might bring more peace, more passion into your life.

Your happiness and joy matter to the health of the world. When you live with happiness and joy arising often, you bring your best self to all that you do; you open inner doorways to your creative nature. As you connect to your creative energy, life suddenly feels like a blank canvas, waiting for you to paint the picture of your life. Creative energy causes you to consider life in new ways, to see the world through your unique lens and ask, what am I here to do and create? What will cause me naturally to serve the world? What talents and gifts do I possess in my deep recesses that can offer something special to the world?

Engage the heart moment-to-moment

Answers to these important questions emerge as you learn to remain in constant connection with your heart wisdom. As you grow strong in tolerating all your emotional states, you also gain understanding about your emotions, and how they may guide you toward your best life.

This is my simple, yet powerful guide to emotions.

- **Anger** lets you know you need to reconsider boundaries. If you act on this truth, your anger dissipates the moment the boundaries are properly placed.

- **Disappointment** lets you know you have created expectations in your mind and heart that have not come to pass. You now need to process this as a loss.

- **Sadness** and **grief** let you know what is important to you, what you value, what you love, and what you want. The loss of anything valuable must be grieved. These emotions teach you how to structure your life for fulfillment.

- **Fear** lets you know you need to grow, gaining skills to step into a greater life.

- **Joy** and **happiness** fuel your being to create goodness in the world, as do passion and excitement.

Understanding these emotions helps you simply allow the energy to move more readily through you, knowing that all emotions pass and new ones come along. Emotional energy is the inner fuel for dancing gracefully and compassionately through life, once you grow the skills of responding authentically, directly and kindly to all you encounter, both within you and around you. The more authentically you respond, the more you gain momentum for living in awareness of what will create more meaning, more passion and more love in your individual life, as well as the lives of those with whom you are connected. You then choose from conscious awareness and an inner creative power, rather than automatically continuing behaviors and thinking that feel negative or destructive. This is how you live your best life. This is how you cultivate peace in your heart. *And it is upon this peace that the subconscious henceforth organizes your life.*

The heart, peace and the subconscious

Affirmations and right thinking are an integral part of creating the quality of life you so desire. And yet affirmations without a foundational belief will not hold you steady when the storms of life arise and create chaos. What *does* offer the stability to weather any chaotic conditions is a heartfelt belief in the goodness and persistence of harmony, truth, love, prosperity, and any and all of the positive qualities you seek. When you believe, not just as a construct in your mind, but literally *feel* the essential strength and power of all things good – harmony, love, prosperity, truth – you are the calm in the storm. You become the organizing influence for that which swirls around you as you hold steady to your inner truths, allowing the rest to fall away. For this to take place, the heart must be engaged in your daily living experience to constantly remind you of life's deepest truths when other ideas and challenges come bumping into your world.

Consider your subconscious as the underlying structure holding the beliefs about life that you *feel* are true. Your original conditioning – that organized your habitual fears, worries, vulnerabilities, and resistances – is the foundation of your life right now. To be a courageous woman and live your inner power, means reconditioning those habitual fears, worries, vulnerabilities, and resistances in a consciously directed manner. You engage your heart regularly to challenge those faulty forces working against what you consciously want to create now. You purposefully develop faith in the goodness, abundance and harmony of life, becoming an organizing force for these qualities to be demonstrated in your life. When you *feel* a lack of harmony, peace or joy, it is inner guidance telling you to work through subconscious beliefs that are still set on faulty structures – those old fears that limit the goodness you deeply desire. As you release the old beliefs, living the truth of harmony and peace, you impact the subconscious of those around you, challenging them to rebuild their faulty, subconscious structures with the qualities you now demonstrate.

Inner Power Practice #17

Notice when you are worrying, or feeling fear and anxiety. Stop and ask yourself what is happening in the present moment that you want to change. Breathe deeply and relax into your heart; practice tapping when the feelings are intense. Ask, how do I need to grow right now? What does my inner being need that I can learn and practice?

The more you engage the heart in your day-to-day living, the more you grow tolerance and compassion for each person and their individual life challenges. You recognize how we are similar and how we are different, but also how, ultimately, we all possess the same qualities. This awareness softens the heart to each individual's plight, each person's challenge to deal with whatever difficulties they face. As your heart softens, it becomes more accepting, more allowing, and kinder. It also grows stronger, more forthright in expressing your truth, willing to share more readily what you feel, since you know 'this feeling too shall pass.' As your heart opens, genuine interest, a curiosity to understand others' experiences from their unique perspective develops. Through this tolerance you become medicine for the world, spreading acceptance, peace, and kindness.

As your strengthening, deepening, heartfelt wisdom expands, returning inward grows to be a natural and joyful habit, allowing you to maintain a clear channel to the Self who offers you and others, wisdom, guidance, inspiration and peace. Let's move into the beautiful practice of returning inward.

Guided relaxation exercise for living through the heart

Sit in a comfortable position. Place your hands gently in your lap with thumbs lightly touching. Place your feet on the floor. Relax your face and your lips. Rest the tip of your tongue gently on the roof of your mouth. Scan your body for tension and direct your breathing to any tightness in your body. Allow your thoughts to flow; imagine them flowing fluidly through you, your mind open to holding a directed thought. Inwardly say, 'My mind is a tool to be directed by me. I focus on what I choose.' Reconnect with your breath and focus your attention on your heart. Imagine yourself breathing into your heart center, letting the breath flow into the rest of your body, infusing you with loving energy. You might choose to see this energy as a golden light, filling your body with the intention to circulate your breath through your heart center.

Notice any disturbance that prevents you bringing this energy into awareness. Invite it to arise more fully into your conscious view. Without judgment or concern, simply look at what presents itself. Breathe into this experience and relax; allow whatever needs to be seen in your mind. Rest with this awareness.

Now gently rest your attention at your heart. Ask yourself what you want. Ask yourself to speak through your heart, to reveal your deepest desires and your simplest wants. Be quiet and still; remain as open and quiet as you can. Repeat the questions. Remain open. Stay with this process as long as you like. When you are ready, return your attention to your breath and open your eyes. Make notes.

To work with your heart in a greater capacity, begin the meditation again or continue after you feel the golden light fully within your being. Breathe into the light and let it soothe and uplift you. Now bring to mind someone you want to send loving energy to, someone you want to heal a relationship with, or someone you know is in need. Imagine yourself breathing out a stream of this beautiful golden light, and let that stream move through space and time to reach the person. Let the light surround and hold them gently in loving energy. Feel your heart expanding to hold them in your energetic embrace of love and kindness. Simply breathe your love and light to them as an offering of healing and kindness. Rest gently in this breathing, holding them in your awareness for however long feels right. When you are ready, follow the golden stream back to where you are, wiggle your fingers and toes, and bring your awareness back into your body. Open your eyes when you are ready and make notes as you wish.

The Inner Power Wheel

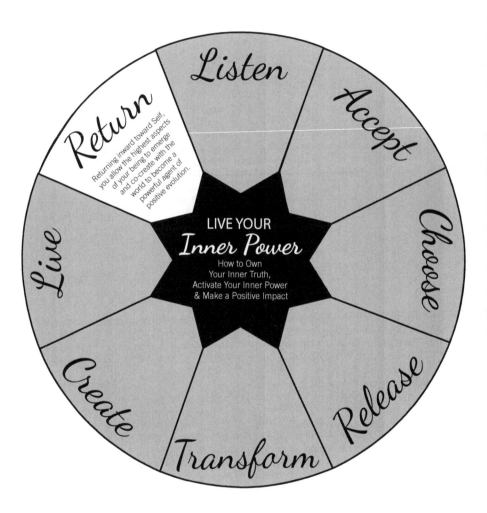

Return — Returning inward toward Self, you allow the highest aspects of your being to emerge and co-create with the world to become a powerful agent of positive evolution.

Listen

Accept

Choose

Release

Transform

Create

Live

LIVE YOUR
Inner Power
How to Own
Your Inner Truth,
Activate Your Inner Power
& Make a Positive Impact

EIGHT

Return Inward

Practice 8: Return

Connecting to, and living in complete harmony with, the truth that waits in inner stillness allows you to take the leap of faith that says 'yes' to life, opening doors to new worlds.

My story

I connect daily to my sacred space within. My inner home is the haven that holds me in sweetness. When I feel challenged, disappointed, frustrated or confused, my inner sanctuary restores me. I discovered this inner place as I learned to sit still with myself.

Daily, I dutifully sat quietly, wanting to get up, frustrated with the process. I took breaks sometimes – never for too long, maybe a few months or a few weeks. From the beginning, I sensed something important shifting as I learned to witness myself. I didn't understand the shift in the early stages; the understanding came later, with the willingness to 'stay with Me, stay with Me, stay with Me.' I wanted to abandon the staying still and just be busy, do life, distract myself from the pangs of loneliness, the waves of frustration, the emotional content that arose when I least expected it.

I wouldn't go back and change one minute of it now. My willingness to commit deeply to seeing Me, holding Me, knowing Me, has taught me how to build a life that brings ultimate joy, peace and fulfillment. *Wow.*

Returning inward was the key to finding the truth that knows how to move my life in directions that feel satisfying in sensual, aesthetic and spiritual ways. I look around and revel at the high-quality, intimate relationships holding me in love and connection every day. These relationships are intimate because now I know me and can share me well. I want to know the other; I want to hold the other in kindness and respect. I learned the tools that bring this into being; I am the co-creator of these wonderful partnerships.

I hold deep appreciation for the home I make with my husband. Our rocky beginning brought profound challenges to creating the family life we now both feel good about and lead as a team. Merging families, especially when a gaggle of grown adults is involved, requires practicing acceptance in its most artful and honest form. For us finally to emerge as leaders of what feels like a family, we had to witness each other's deepest truth.

I could stay still and discover mine – not always easy when conflicting desires press at the psyche. But the willingness to stay with the process, to turn the medicine wheel again and again and discover what holds me back from living in joy, this is the beauty of the Inner Power wheel. The joy is always available: the question becomes, how am I keeping myself away from joy? What am I trying to control instead of flow with? This discovery is made when I return inward and listen into the stillness. Answers, insights, *my knowing* continues to flow.

Meditation and contemplation as a path to truth

Life direction is just one of the many benefits of meditation, self-reflection and contemplation. The wonders that come through sitting with Self expand exponentially for me as time passes; what started out as a curiosity about meditation has blossomed into a way of life that consistently returns insight, empowerment, and peace.

Adding morning meditation and contemplation to my routine wasn't always easy – like many, I battled resistance. Thankfully, my persistence won the battle. I feel grounded, clear and purposeful as I head into each day, after communing with Self first thing in the morning.

In the beginning, I focused on breath meditation as I learned the skill of sitting still with myself for twenty minutes or more. I battled to stay still and not itch to get up; it was hard to resist the inner voice that came up with every important thing I needed to do – right away – instead of sitting with Self. After some consistent communing with my big Self, which is always a pleasure, I found it much easier to remain on the cushion or in the chair.

For me, communing with big Self entails connecting with the inner voice of knowing. As I learned to quiet my mind for brief periods (a minute was a big success!), what I called 'knowings' began to occur. Call it intuition, call it my soul communicating, call it spirit speaking, call it anything – but I call it a 'knowing' because it's self-explanatory. My 'knowings' felt like assurance about something I was wondering about. Suddenly, I would have insight on how to proceed, what the deeper issue was that challenged me, or what communication was needed. As I trusted these 'knowings' and took action, life became easier; there was less struggling as more and more good things took form in my world. These 'knowings' became a catalyst for wanting more experience of sitting with Self.

My morning meditation usually begins silently, as I sit with the breath, refocusing again and again on my inner experience, retracting attention from my thoughts. I hold the vision of the dream life I continue to create, moving through one positive and exciting experience onto the next. Life has become a canvas on which I paint my personal vision – the image of Life as I want to experience it. Prayer time is now part of the experience, as I learn to give voice to my grateful heart for all the goodness and love in my life, to commune with the great Creative Force, to claim what my heart yearns for. I ask to be the agent of change and creative healing as I imagine my world, and the world around me, in the greatest harmony my limited imagination can call forth. And finally, I may include movement and coordinated breath-work as I transition from sitting in stillness to moving into my day. Adding meditative movement sets the pace of my day and launches me in peaceful rhythm with life around me.

This daily contemplation time has evolved from my earlier focus on healing inner distress and unrest (there were many years of this), to sitting and seeking clarity about my motivations, intentions and desires. Now it's much about giving thanks for the good that has come and holding my vision in clarity. The healing process was important, because it opened me to inner wisdom and clarity that was clouded by my inner distress. Now, as clarity becomes a more consistent way of life, I find my morning routine tends to be about aligning my inner world – thought, word and deed – to live as a creative agent in the world. My morning quiet is about sitting in the grace of living consciously and intentionally, in awareness of the inner peace and love that arises through living with self-awareness.

Connect inwardly as a way of life

The more you create the habit of connecting inwardly, especially in stillness, the stronger your inner connection becomes. As you travel the medicine wheel of *Courageous Woman, Live Your Inner Power*, you become aware of the power you hold within to become a creative force in the world. And through this awareness, your creative energy knows no limits.

When I first started my path through the wheel of *Courageous Woman, Live Your Inner Power*, I was confused and disappointed with life in many ways. My connection to what my inner self knew was right and true for me was lost amid the 'shoulds' and 'musts' of living the life path I had started down. Finally, I let myself honor my wake-up calls, which – although hard to hear – were asking me to stop and take stock of what I had chosen thus far. I began to consider how my past had driven me, how fear of judgment and loss had guided important choices, and how disconnection from my heart was literally making me sick. This was a lot to process and to accept as the result of my personal choices. Choosing to honor what I knew was my truth was scary, and took time and courage to achieve.

Tolerating sitting quietly was difficult in those days. I had to let myself feel feelings that I had walled off. It was time to acknowledge thoughts I had only allowed to lurk around the edges of my consciousness, thoughts of my truth. It felt uncomfortable to accept that I was afraid and confused about what to do. I had no plan for how to make it right, how to make changes, how to speak my truth to those I knew I needed to share those thoughts with. First, I had to learn to sit with myself and accept that I had made these choices and I had reasons for doing so, even if they went against my deep inner voice of knowing. My perfectionist streak kept whirling me around in a cycle of acceptance, judgment and feelings of failure. I had a difficult time accepting I had simply made choices that weren't in my highest good, or the good of those with whom I was in relationship. But my compassionate nature eventually turned itself towards me, and let my whole story be present and accounted for. I simply sat with the truth of it all.

And slowly, as I began to speak the truth of my feelings, sharing the real inner me, others came to know me better. I made new decisions, both for myself and others with whom I had co-created to that point. I gave those decisions time to evolve naturally as we all shared our truth and spoke from the heart. Changes were made, difficult choices put into play, losses grieved, and much releasing of the past processed. These were cycles of emotions that needed to be lived through with a patient and kind heart for everyone involved. I really grew my heart muscles in those days. I learned how much grieving I could bear for unconscious choices made from fear and a sense of powerlessness. There was much forgiveness work to do, particularly in forgiving myself for what I saw as my failure in having made choices that impacted others' lives so profoundly. Patience and time allowed me to emerge with a renewed sense of hope for a future where I would choose more consciously and honorably, listening to the wisdom of my inner world.

Inner Power Practice #18

Choose an area of your life where you desire change. Explore your feelings openly with a trusted other, becoming deeply honest about your wants. Do not take action. Begin to share your deeper, honest feelings with those involved. Do not make decisions or do anything – simply share feelings and truth. Try this consciously for one month and take notice of any shifts that occur.

My new boundaries intact and learning to live in new ways, I stepped carefully forward to create a life in tune with the Self I was getting to know more intimately. It was both exhilarating and frightening at times. I was learning to tune into my heart moment-to-moment, to put into practice the compassion I had developed, to take steps consistently in line with my heartfelt truth. I had to learn how to say no in new ways, and to say yes to things I would have been too timid to walk towards in the past. The art of setting healthy, flexible boundaries became a way of life.

And always it is time to turn inward again, to hear the call of what my Self knows I can grow into next, how I can contribute in new ways to the goodness in the world and become a healing agent of change. The inner world has consistently guided me well. I trust, I trust.

Bring your deeper self to the present moment

Through this trust, you create a springboard that allows you to leap towards what your heart and being crave. By sitting in daily quiet, communing with the stillness in and around you, you grow a strong connection to the deeper aspects of yourself. You become able to bring that inner awareness of deep connection to Self, who is calm, clear and compassionate, into your daily experience. It is this calm inner peace experienced in quiet time that you intentionally make available, in a more steady state, in your daily round, consciously creating a peaceful quality of experience no matter what chaos may be happening around you. You are the calm in the storms of life. This is how you develop the capacity to be an agent of healing and change to the world around you simply through your presence. This is powerful medicine for you and for others.

As awareness develops, you become sensitive to how you connect with others, and the energy around you. Your awareness expands to take more in, allowing it all, simply being with what is around you without having to do anything, to judge or control anything. You have learned the art of allowing whatever arises in and around as you practice sitting still, through growing the muscles of tolerance. You experience life more as pure energy, rather than processing everything as stories, through thoughts, words and concepts. You hold space around you without needing to impose ideas or judgments of any kind.

You are simply the observer. What freedom there is in this kind of being! What relief from needing answers, having to tell a story, or know a *reason* for anything! Instead you enjoy simply being present to the moment. You naturally begin to move towards what your inner being wants, and away from that which does not appeal to, connect with or attract you. You feel you are flowing with life naturally. You grow trust in life itself.

Inner Power Practice #19

Practice being the observer. Use all your senses to bring you into the present experience. Focus on the sensual experience, versus the story of what is happening. See if you can let go of 'structuring' responses, simply seeing what arises. Do not judge the experience, simply note what is.

Tune in beyond your five senses

As you grow trust in life itself, you relax into its flow including the truth that life – as you know it – will end one day. And you become comfortable with this notion as you experience the feeling that you are more than your body, something impossible to fully comprehend through a mental process. By moving the mind chatter out of the way, you discover *a sense of 'more than body.'* Because it is difficult to quiet the mind, you may miss the opportunity to revel in tuning in to soul/spirit; this higher vibration happens through commitment, effort and practice.

Paradoxically, experiencing a sense of being more than the body can come through paying attention to the body. Redirecting attention from mental activity to awareness of breath and bodily sensations can be a portal for slipping quietly and effortlessly into a sense of expansiveness –the sensation that you are more than just your body. Developing trust through experiences that open your mind and inner awareness to wisdom about your Self is powerful medicine for you. Through this high vibration, you can grow a feeling of faith about life.

Journal Inventory #20

Write your own life philosophy. Let it answer important questions about purpose and meaning. What do you think life is for? What do you believe we humans are here to discover and learn? How do you approach life as a whole? What is the point to this dance we call life?

Write from the heart, going back to explore the questions

further. Continue writing and refining for at least a month as you let the questions sink deeper into your conscious and subconscious mind. Post this somewhere you can see it regularly. The purpose is to find the inner truth that will bring you comfort in times of trouble.

To have faith means you rely on a set of principles or beliefs that guide you when life seems uncertain and challenging; they govern your individual and personal inner experience. Faith allows you to flow more readily with life's journey. You establish faith by adopting a mindset of faith – a clear belief in your optimal potential.

Opening inwardly to a dimension of life beyond physical expression is an option open to you and to everyone by remaining in a state of receptivity. Meditation and attuning to stillness, in conjunction with an examination of your mind-made beliefs, offer an opportunity to experience this dynamic receptivity.

Knowing your mind's limitations, as well as its strengths, deepens your experience of life. Thoughts fueled by feelings may be impassioned thoughts, but are still simply thoughts, created in the mind. Testing your thoughts through treating them as ideas rather than facts, gives you a chance to discover the truth about them. Recognize your power over your thoughts and beliefs as you examine them through directed attention and experimentation. Open to the power of wonder!

To know life beyond the input of your five senses and mind is an opportunity afforded to all. You must invite yourself to the experience of *more*. When you do this consciously and consistently, results follow. Ultimately, you invite a higher attunement when you say yes to any experience that seems mysterious, beyond explanation by the mind. Seeking a deeper knowing of that which exists beyond your limited body-self, connects your consciousness to what seems like a limitless resource – you open the door, and tell the world, 'I am ready for more.'

Coming full circle

I love how the practices of *Courageous Woman, Live Your Inner Power* represent a wheel of life that forever continues. Once you have made your way around the wheel, you return to where you began. As you travel the wheel and listen to your wake-up calls, answering to life as it calls on you to become all you can be, the calls become less about distress and more about adventure and meaning. You are called to experience your highest potential in this lifetime.

As you develop a strong connection to your heart and learn to live consistently through the heart, you understand that your capacity to grow and learn about life is limited only by your choice. Your strengthening heart connection reminds you that universal love as a guiding energy is far greater than your individual oneness, despite the importance of developing your unique capacities and talents. It is through this ever-expanding love, sensing yourself as part of this enormous energy, that you feel humbled by the greatness of life itself. And it is through your ability to tune in and return to this all-pervading connection within that you feel called to continue this life journey of your own individual greatness.

Tune in to your higher gifts: the lifetime journey

And so it is that you return again and again inwardly, tuning in and discovering where else Life wants you to go and what else Life wants you to know about. Through this connection within Self, you feel called to experience more life, more love and more meaning. As this inner connection strengthens, life develops into an amazing adventure, calling you into the fullness of who you are at your very essence. You are Courageous Woman, living your inner power, and you are medicine to the world.

Guided relaxation exercise
for tuning in beyond your five senses

Sit comfortably and attune to your breath. Place your hands gently in your lap with thumbs lightly touching. Place your feet on the floor. Relax your face and your lips. Rest the tip of your tongue gently on the roof of your mouth. Scan your body for tension and direct your breathing to any tightness in your body. Allow your thoughts to flow fluidly through you, sensing that your mind is open to holding a directed thought. Inwardly say, 'My mind and awareness are tools to be directed by me. I focus on what I choose. I direct my mind where I want it to be.' Reconnect with your breath and focus your attention on your heart. Imagine yourself breathing into your heart center and letting the breath flow from there into the rest of your body, infusing you with loving energy. See this energy as a golden light filling your body, circulating through your heart center with each breath and then throughout every cell of your body. Sense the energy of your inner world, the quiet that is there when you become still and tune in to it. Bring your attention to the crown of your head and imagine a stream of white light pouring in, cascading into your being and filling all the cells of your body. Hold the image of you sitting still, with this light coming from somewhere above. You are the receptacle of this light, this energy. Bask in your sense of receiving this light and warmth. Feel your body tingling with the high vibration of this energy. Stay still for as long as you can, enjoying this powerful energetic source of Life. When you are ready, offer heartfelt thanks for the experience. Refocus your attention on your breath and gently open your eyes. Make notes.

The Inner Power Wheel

Listen

Listen to the wake up calls that come from within and develop tolerance and understanding for these important messages. They hold the keys to your deep healing.

Accept

Acceptance is the foundational platform from which all change launches. Patterns of resistance create toxic conditions within the body and form blocks to truth and power.

Return

Returning inward toward Self, you allow the highest aspects of your being to emerge and co-create with the world to become a powerful agent of positive evolution.

Choose

Choosing consciously allows you to create the personal destiny you most desire. With conscious choice you align with the present moment and grow response-ability.

Live

Clear thinking, balanced with heart wisdom, is power. In learning to live through the heart, your lens of perception is filtered through your profound connection to the ultimate source.

LIVE YOUR Inner Power

How to Own Your Inner Truth, Activate Your Inner Power & Make a Positive Impact

Release

Releasing the past's limitations translates to growing in your present power and fully accessing the truth of today. This unburdening opens you to the present moment.

Create

With consciousness of bringing life into form through, you, you choose carefully your inner and outer boundaries. This practice harnesses energy and power in service to your desires.

Transform

Transforming losses into pearls of wisdom turns lead into gold, the alchemist's path. Shedding accumulated grief frees you to tap into your essential wisdom and open to joy.

CLOSING

The *Inner Power* medicine wheel turns in your inner world constantly once you have mastered all the practices as a way of life. Each practice feels like a gift you give to yourself and others. Like me, you can't help but invite others to bring the wheel into their own life and experience its profound impact, transforming life into a consciously directed flow. Let's recap the wheel and how it lives within you.

Listening and responding to that which calls from you becomes natural, even if it is uncomfortable, at first, to turn towards the feelings and energy within. Each wake-up call helps you grow into more of what your heart longs for, more of what your soul searches for.

Acceptance is a gift to yourself and others. With consistent acceptance, trust in both yourself and the world around you develops organically, creating a foundation for living forward, instead of going backwards or stalling.

As you choose more consciously, with awareness of your inner world as well as your outer experience, you develop confidence in yourself and how the world supports your highest good with a flow that feels natural and authentic. Feeling the power you hold in being the creator of your experience often swings between freeing and frightening! You learn to ride the wave of exhilaration this brings.

Releasing the past is an ongoing stripping of layers of beliefs handed down to you, a letting go of habits stimulated by negativity and fear, rather than love and goodness. As you release again and again, you feel more present to the moment, no longer burdened by the 'shoulds' and 'musts' that once restrained you. You free yourself to live in the now, wherein lies your ability to choose in alignment with your deep truth.

Transforming grief into personal pearls of wisdom builds an inner toolbox you can rely on when times are troubling. The wisdom that emerges after grief, earned through experience, becomes your bedrock as you engage fully with life and face any difficulties that arise.

Creating healthy boundaries becomes your artist's brush as you choose powerfully and carefully where to put your time and attention, where to give your energy and love, what to invite into your world and what to move on from. Your movable boundaries are like riverbanks, the rush of your life energy unstoppable as it gushes forth to meet the world.

The heart becomes your inner resting place to dive ever more deeply into the truth of what you want, who you are becoming, and how to bring your unique gifts and energy into the world. Feeling powerfully in tune with your heart energy will grow your compassionate nature, turning you into a gentle, but powerful force of goodness and light in the world.

Returning inward causes the beautiful wheel of consciously bold living to continue turning in your life. As you live in this model of high co-creation with life, you naturally share these practices with those around you. The energy of your personal creativity beneficially influences and inspires the people with whom you connect.

How does this sound? Too good to be true? It's not. I am living proof, along with my many clients and life-mates that this wheel works to transform your life into precisely what you want. In time, you find you are living the great adventure of your life as you co-create with the world around you, while honoring that which your deepest Self desires. Trust grows as you discover that your deep inner self does indeed know what will fulfill and sustain you.

Your mind, now reconditioned to be alert to the present, becomes the servant of your heart and soul's desires. Your transformative mental energy serves the world when you practice observing your thoughts, and aligning your thinking with what is of great importance to you. You no longer feel like a puppet in a drama you don't want to be in. Instead, you are the director and the hero or heroine of your play – *My Life*, the most important play you will ever star in.

When you find yourself stagnant or frustrated, disheartened or confused, learn to sit patiently with the feelings for a time. Turn the wheel of *Courageous Woman, Live Your Inner Power*. Pose questions to which you may not immediately know the answers, and allow them to work into your deeper consciousness. Questions you might pose include:

- What am I turning away from? What wake-up call am I ignoring?
- How am I resisting what is happening right now? How do I need to embrace acceptance?
- What reactive, automatic behaviors, thoughts and feelings am I experiencing right now?
- What is happening that may be a version of my past?
- What grief am I avoiding?
- What boundaries am I reluctant to set?
- How am I ignoring what my heart wants?
- How am I connecting inwardly, and if I am not, how am I avoiding this?
- If I could change this aspect of my life, immediately, what would change?

To sit in stillness with whatever arises within you, observe it, hold it gently with wonder at what you are experiencing – this is the great gift of *Courageous Woman, Live Your Inner Power*. When you can sit in stillness with Self, you are not unconsciously driven in ways that do not serve you and the world in the highest manner. Instead, you condition your unconscious mind to support you in claiming your heart's desires in tune with life around you. You align your thinking and behaviors with these deep desires. You passionately live a life of purpose and meaning, fulfilled and enlivened by your experiences every day. This is medicine for the world.

So what can you do to bring this wheel alive in your life and transform your daily experience into crafting the life you deeply desire, with conscious presence and a bold heart? Focus on each of the practices intensely for at least one month. Hone your skill level by holding each practice alive and active in your everyday experience. Visit www.laurelhh.com to see when the next *Live Your Inner Power* Program begins and enjoy support while taking the journey with others.

Take each challenge in your life today and work with it through the Inner Power wheel. Be on the look-out for other challenging situations and consider them through the lens of the wheel of practices. When difficulties arise, journal answers to each of the following questions and see what valuable information arises. The answers provide the needed guidance for action that feels authentically powerful and true to you.

- What might be the wake-up call in this situation?
- What are you resisting – what don't you like about this that you can accept?
- If you close your eyes and ask yourself, 'what do I want in this?' – what is the first thing that arises?
- What are you aware of energetically in this experience? How are you reactive?
- Is there a loss associated with anything that's happening here?
- What boundary do you need to help you move through this experience?
- How is your heart feeling about what is going on? Name any emotions.

- Take time for stillness and turn inward to simply hold this experience in wonder; ask, 'how is this challenge serving me?'
- How does this challenge want you to grow?

Pose these questions regularly and see how transformative they can be as you consider how to proceed and how to identify your choices and what you really want.

And finally, a little more encouragement for exploring the wheel:

- Remember, the goal is to move into the territory of feeling more open, ready to access endless life possibilities.
- Search relentlessly for the inner and outer messages that limit your ability to love yourself. Replace them with updated messages that affirm your inner journey.
- Grow to believe you deserve the best life can offer.
- Take a breath and pay attention to your thoughts.
- Take a breath and pay attention to your heart.
- Understand how your mind automatically moves in particular directions.
- Remember that your mind is under your control.
- Practice re-directing thoughts to focus on your consciously chosen themes.
- Dismantle the old internal structure that holds you where you do not want to be.
- Find support to do the work of releasing past history so you no longer focus in the reverse direction.
- Utilize a support system that empowers you and supports your deepest yearnings.
- Review your relationships regularly, keeping in mind the possible need for altered boundaries as you grow and change.

- Reconsider each relationship in your life as you choose to be healthier, and focus on creation vs. stagnation.

- Create space in your daily schedule to be with the inner journey.

- Slow the intensity of the process if you feel tired by too much change happening too fast.

- Listen to your words every moment, searching for your own limiting messages.

- Learn to trust yourself through daily actions that are in line with your inner truth.

- Remember to focus on the positive in order to increase those aspects of your life.

- Turn inward and listen as often as possible.

I would love to support you further in your inner journey. You can connect with me via email at laurelhollandh@gmail.com. You can subscribe to my *Live Your Inner Power* newsletter and find links to videos and articles that support and encourage your ongoing journey, as you learn about and master living through your inner world. Before you know it, you will powerfully manifest what your heart desires in your daily reality.

I am honored that you brought *Courageous Woman, Live Your Inner Power* into your world through this reading. My wish is for you to experience the passion and joy that crafting your life with conscious presence and a bold heart offers. May you go forth to discover what fulfills you, and bring your special gifts to the world. Blessings and love to you.

HOW TO FURTHER ACTIVATE THE INNER POWER WHEEL IN AND AROUND YOU

I like to imagine what transformations might take place as more people live with the practices of the Inner Power Wheel. I see individuals more awake to the infinite possibility of personal creativity that can manage or alleviate many of the problems of the world. In my mind, I see fewer people suffering as they liberate themselves from unconscious patterns that self-perpetuate. I imagine the world as more loving and more harmonious.

You can continue your journey with the Inner Power Wheel. Please visit my website, www.laurelhh.com, for more details. For those wanting to connect with others who are consciously learning and practicing the Inner Power Practices, you can participate in the Live Your Inner Power Program. Currently I hold the program in the Richmond Virginia area. An on-line program is planned for 2015.

For individuals who want to incorporate the Inner Power Wheel into their work to use with your team, your community group, or even your family, teacher training begins in 2015. Please contact me if you are interested. The training provides group leadership skills that can benefit all areas of your life, from relationships, to group and team dynamics. We all benefit when others take expanded responsibility for the environments within which we live and work. The Inner Power Wheel is an empowering path to that shift. My contact information is

Cell phone: 804-241-2831

Email: laurelhollandh@gmail.com

I hope to connect with you personally and support you further in your personal and professional development! If our life journeys do not connect us in person, I send you love and light for all things good and joyful in your life. Thank you for taking this time with me and being a part of my world.

Made in the USA
Middletown, DE
17 July 2015